NIGEL TRANTER'S
SCOTLAND

NIGEL TRANTER'S
SCOTLAND

A VERY PERSONAL REVIEW

BY NIGEL TRANTER

RICHARD DREW PUBLISHING

FIRST PUBLISHED 1981
© NIGEL TRANTER 1981

PUBLISHED BY
RICHARD DREW PUBLISHING LIMITED
MOLENDINAR PRESS
20 PARK CIRCUS, GLASGOW G3 6BE

ISBN 0 904002 73 X

DESIGNED BY JAMES W. MURRAY
SET IN CHELTENHAM BOOK
PRINTED AND BOUND BY
BUTLER AND TANNER LIMITED
FROME AND LONDON

FOREWORD

The object in putting pen to paper thus is simple of design if somewhat complex in operation perhaps. I have thought to set down my own very personal views and ideas about Scotland and the Scots, and how I have been involved in trying, on occasion, to do something about them both and their problems – very modest efforts, to be sure, diverse and not always judicious nor yet successful; but well-meant and consistent at least in the ultimate aim.

So this is not a panegyric on Scotland's bonny braes and couthy folk, nor yet a coffee-table picturebook nor tourist's guide. Nor is it an autobiography. It is merely one man's somewhat incoherent but quite strongly-held notions about his own country and his fellow-citizens, some interpretations of its long and bloody story, and some account of certain of his experiences in rashly seeking to paddle now and again in the drumly waters of Scots affairs and problems, social, practical, cultural, even mildly political.

Writers are apt to be busybodies, all in the cause of authenticity and suitable involvement, of course, that they may write with the more authority – or that is the usual excuse; and I am no exception. What follows is no academic exercise nor thesis, merely something of a rag-bag of observations, convictions and propositions. It is not meant to be presumptuous – so, if it may occasionally seem so, forgive!

CONTENTS

chapter one
THE LAND

I have never wanted to live anywhere else than in Scotland – and the pressures to do so upon authors, for tax-avoidance, are quite strong. But although I have travelled to far places and seen many other countries, and often much liked what I saw, it is Scotland for me, where I was born, brought up, lived my life, met my challenges and joys, failures and pains, delights and disappointments, all of them in good measure. For that, of course, is living; and Scotland is a place apt for full living, a land of heights and depths, of contrasts and exaggerations, of aching beauty and sheer damnable ugliness, of poetry and the most prosaic prose imaginable, of the excellent and the very bad. In fact, a country of extremes, in land as in people – which is rather ironic, considering how the Scots like to describe themselves as God's most solid, competent, down-to-earth, reliable and well-doing creation, a worthy model for less favoured folk; whereas in fact they are a race of argumentative extremists and sentimental softies, with a genius for invention, religious disputation, metaphysics and disunity, brilliant at minding successfully other folk's business but not their own. And the land itself has much to do with all this, undoubtedly.

Duncansby Head with the Little Stack and the Muckle Stack

Just look at it, on any map of any scale you like. Have you ever seen a more ridiculously unbalanced geographical entity? It is all awkward angles and corners; land and water hopelessly entangled, bits thrusting out into the sea for miles and miles, the sea probing into the land still more so; mountains and hills all over the place, yet with some of the richest agricultural land in Europe; all the best parts practically empty, the worst parts overflowing with population; crazily lop-sided, with its east coast of only some five hundred miles while the west runs into thousands; with seven-hundred-and-eighty-seven islands sufficiently large to be so-called; three fifths the size of England yet with only four cities and one-tenth of the population. And so on. Can you wonder if its people are less than level-headed, whatever their world-wide reputation – always remembering that there are four times as many Scots overseas as in Scotland?

So this is the land which I, for one, could not do without. For one aspect of it all is certain, to be relied on, built-in – Scotland is never dull.

Back to the map again. Even a fairly superficial glance will reveal certain basic features, unbalanced as they are. Firstly there is a vast dichotomy between the east and the west, in more than the coastline – and this applies to the people as well as the land. There are a great deal more Highlands than Lowlands; yet this is not just a matter of north and south, as is often assumed. In fact the Lowlands continue up to Aberdeenshire and beyond, and the Highlands reach down almost to Glasgow and to the Mull of Kintyre – further south incidentally than Alnwick in Northumberland. And while we are at this comparison of latitudes and longitudes, be it noted that the most southerly part of Scotland, the Mull of Galloway, is further south than Durham, and that Manchester is further east than Edinburgh, whilst Ardnamurchan Point, the most westerly spot in mainland Scotland, is further west than Belfast. But what is important to Scotland's story is that the agricultural land is almost all on the east side. And that south of the Forth and Clyde estuaries – which come to within thirty miles of each other, a notable 'waist' of the land – although there are a lot of hills, there is really very little comparison with the Highland area. South Scotland is diversified, with rich farming countryside, great city complexes, rolling grassy uplands, fertile valleys, industrial towns, ancient estates, mining areas, villages and lonely sheep-strewn hills. The more north-easterly provinces of Fife and Angus, the Mearns and much of Aberdeenshire, are scarcely similar but of something of the same character. Whereas the huge Highland area is utterly different, admittedly varying somewhat between the east and central Highlands and the still more colourful west, but still an entity. Here are

Two of the Three Sisters, Glencoe

great rugged mountains and endless ranges of heather hills, mighty rushing, peat-brown rivers in narrow glens or broad straths, lochs by the thousand, vast forests and vaster moors and a seaboard to dream over – and respect. But there are precious few towns and villages, and out of Scotland's five million population not one in twenty live beyond the Highland Line – although it was by no means always so. This division and imbalance must never be forgotten, for on it hinges much of Scotland's fate. The islands, of course, the Hebrides and the Orcades, are a story unto themselves.

I stress all this geography and topography because it has had –

and still has – its powerful effect on me and on my life. As indeed it has, consciously or otherwise, on nearly all Scots. I, for one, have always been very much aware of the land, its differences and delights, its character and its challenges – and its reproaches. For much of our lovely land is a standing reproach to this and previous generations. I have visited every single parish in mainland Scotland, and more than visited, explored and examined them in some depth. I have walked every area of the country – save for the Outer Hebrides and Shetland. I have savoured and assessed and contemplated every reach and corner of this most extraordinary and dramatic land – I have had to, for my books on its castles and the countryside – and love it all. Whether I really *know* it all, of course is another matter. I do not, I'm afraid. But at least I know enough to recognise that the folk on it are scarcely worthy of the land – and yet I love the folk too, myself being admittedly as unworthy as any. When I think of all the things I once thought to do with and for it, and have done so little . . . !

Before I try to set down some small hint of the impact of the various parts of Scotland upon myself, as upon others, natives and visitors both, it is surely valid to say something about the climate. For the climate moulds the land – and has its own effect upon the inhabitants undoubtedly. And Scotland's climate is as unbalanced and diverse as its topography, and as misrepresented quite often. There is a belief much held beyond our borders that Scotland is a cold wet place, much afflicted by snow and ice, indeed a sort of suburb of the Arctic regions. The fact is that there is no such thing as Scottish weather. The differences in climatic conditions in various parts of the country are pronounced. East Lothian, for instance, where I live, is one of the driest areas of the British Isles, more so than say the South-East of England; and Dunbar, our easternmost town, is renowned for consistently having more sunshine than almost anywhere else – except, perhaps, the Isle of Tiree in the Inner Hebrides, strangely enough. On the other hand, we do suffer from cold winds off the North Sea and at certain seasons the chill gloomy easterly haars, or sea-mists, which can play the devil with all but the bone-headed. The west of the country is wetter than the east but with slightly higher temperatures. And of course, the West Highland seaboard is largely sub-tropical, thanks to the Gulf Stream – or, as we must now call it, I understand, the North Atlantic Drift – which here curls in and helps to produce that extraordinary concentration of beauty and colour and clarity of atmosphere, which is unsurpassed in heart-breaking loveliness when the sun shines on the Hebridean Sea, caused by the multi-hued seaweeds of the rocks and skerries, the brilliant white sands formed by ground-up cockle-shells, the clear amethyst and blue-green water, the floral carpeting of the sandy machars, and the rich vegetation where there is soil enough to sustain it. Palms grow along the coast, to the astonishment of visitors, and some of the finest and most spectacular gardens in the land are in the Highland West, the most famous at Inverewe in Wester Ross and at Acha-more on the Isle of Gigha. Snow is almost unknown in many parts. Other areas have quite different weather patterns, to be sure, with more snow perhaps in the Central Highlands than elsewhere, chill winds on the Aberdeenshire and Mearns coasts, general salubrity in the Laigh of Moray, and more rain in Galloway, say, than in Lothian. By and large Scotland's weather is a deal better than often suggested – and we seldom suffer from airless, enervating heat. I know no part where fresh air is in any short supply!

Inevitably I have my favourite parts of the land, for varying reasons. Perhaps some examples will reveal something of my attitudes and preferences. Certainly the Borderland, to start at the south, ranks high by any standards, a territory quite distinct from all the rest, even in these days of mass-influences and creeping sameness. It is, of course, divided traditionally into East, Middle and West Marches, as beloved of the ballads; and indeed there are still differences, especially between the East and Middle as against the West March. It is all, however, a fair green land of hills and valleys and great rivers, of ruined abbeys and peel towers, of busy woollen-mill towns, old estates with famous names and large farms whereon not only fine cattle and sheep pasture but horses prolifer-

Galashiels Common Riding

ate, clean-limbed riding-horses. This is most noticeable in an age when the horse has become something of a rarity except as a riding-school adjunct; and is explained by two causes, one preponderant – the Common Riding phenomenon and the foxhunting. It is the former which interests me, and most Borderers.

You see, practically every Border town and sizeable community in the East and Middle Marches has its annual Common or March Riding festival, some of very ancient origin, some comparatively modern, but all pursued with great gusto and panache – and the horse takes a very prominent part in all. The festivals, modelled on those of Hawick and Selkirk – if I dare say so – seem to derive their inspiration from the national disaster of the Battle of Flodden, of 1513, when the over-chivalrous James the Fourth led the flower of his land to defeat and death in a quite unnecessary invasion of England, as a gallant gesture towards the Queen of France who had sent her glove as token and challenge – a fairly typically unbalanced Scottish sentimental ploy, if I may say so, and something the more level-headed English would never have contemplated. Very few of the heroes returned – but the Town Clerk of Selkirk did, lawyers usually being noted for discretion – and Selkirk has been celebrating the fact ever since; whilst Hawick, its rival, takes its festival's origin from the year after, 1514 when, with the border wide open to assault by any enterprising English, a raiding band of the Northumbrian Prior of Hexham's minions were ambushed and wiped out by Hawick youths one June night – all the adult men having failed to come home from Flodden. But just to ensure that Selkirk does not crow too loudly about being first in the field, as it were, Hawick shrewdly back-dates its affair safely into the mists of antiquity by including in the ceremonies – which go on almost for a week – a celebration to greet the sunrise, harking back to Pictish sun-worship.

This rivalry is to be emphasised, with all the other burghs, Jedburgh, Kelso, Galashiels, Langholm, Melrose, Duns, Coldstream, Lauder and the rest, vying with each other in lively and picturesque ongoings, in which large numbers of enthusiasts on horseback, in the old Border reiving tradition, dash from one place to another, with stirrup-cups in between, along with other activities of course. These last include the need for oratory of a sort – which is where I came in, being no equestrian, nor orator either, to be honest. Hawick started it all by asking me to pontificate at one of their exhausting events; and after that, many of the others followed suit and I went the rounds of the Common Ridings for a number of years, until they all had had quite enough of me.

The point about rehearsing all this is that three novels developed out of it, *Cheviot Chase*, *Balefire* and *The Night Riders*.

The last rather highlights the matter for me. I had observed that although all the Scots Border burghs held these annual festivals, none of their English counterparts did so – which seemed strange, so comparatively near-at-hand and sharing the same history from a different angle. Then, doing the Redeswire oration at the Jedburgh Riding one year, an Englishman came up to me and declared that all this was nothing but xenophobia – if I knew what the word meant! All just the Scots giving themselves a cheer. I answered with great dignity – but later thought about it all and decided that the wretched man had something there. So there and then I resolved to try to amend the situation. With two friends I made a tour through the English borderland, forcing myself upon mayors and local dignitaries to try to convince them that they ought to be doing something of the sort and that at least they should come to see what went on at these Scottish affairs – since the theme was all about Scots-English confrontation – and then perhaps go and set up Common Ridings of their own. After all, they mostly had common lands too. I'm afraid that I achieved only two successes, no doubt appearing a complete crank to the rest – the good Mayor of Morpeth and the Chairman of the Hexham Rural District Council, who rashly allowed themselves to get involved with the Jedburgh and Hawick ploys respectively. It was a great joy and satisfaction to me when next year, a Morpeth contingent duly attended at the Carter Bar for the Redeswire celebrations – only in cars, admittedly, but in subsequent years on horseback, as their ancestors had done, in rather different mood. Something achieved – the English also giving themselves a cheer!

Enough of my involvement as an adoptive Borderer. Except to confess that I have never managed to feel quite the same way about the West March, strangely, despite the excitements of the Dumfries Guid Nychburris festival, the magnetism of the Debateable Lands, the Bruce-Comyn drama here, and my fascination with Hermitage Castle. My loss, to be sure.

I have loved East Lothian enough to make it my home for over forty years, this northerly neighbour of the Borders beyond the

Gullane Bay, looking east

Lammermuirs. I was born in Glasgow but brought to Edinburgh at the age of four and reared there, educated, if that is the word, at the ancient George Heriot's School, and first set up house and home there. But, although I have a great regard for the Capital of Scotland, its dignity, its beauties – and the reverse – and its resounding story, I am not a man for cities; and so as soon as I began to see the possibility of my little family being able to actually live on my pen, I upped sticks and went to drive them in again sixteen miles eastwards along the shores of the Firth of Forth, at Aberlady.

The Lothians may be an entity, but the three of them are very different in character – especially East, or Haddingtonshire as it used to be known. It is a lovely, rich land, with thousand upon thousands of acres of the best soil in Scotland, prosperous huge farms with rents to raise the eyebrows, each with its farm-toun of cottages, pleasant brown-stone, red-roofed villages amongst old trees, and but four burghs, industry confined to a small western corner. It is divided into three parallel corridors, east and west; the

coastal plain, with land almost worth its weight in gold; the central
strath, which is basically the fair Vale of Tyne, almost as fertile; and
the green upland terrain of the Lammermuir foothills, sheep and
cattle country. Lower, the land is on the whole far too valuable for
livestock.

Oddly enough it was ducks which brought me to East Lothian –
wild ducks. Although that is not quite accurate, for I married my
dear May in the village kirk of Athelstaneford, in a hanging-valley
between the Vales of Peffer and Tyne, a sequestered, old-world
village where our daughter and her family now live. But it was six
years before we came from Edinburgh to live at Aberlady. In those
days I was a keen shooting-man, and Aberlady Bay is a great place
for wild-ducks and wild-geese, its fifteen-hundred acres of mud-
flats, sand-bars, saltmarsh and dune-country the haunt of wildfowl
and waders innumerable. So I was apt to spend quite a lot of my
free time travelling to and from Aberlady; and May, who had a
blessedly practical streak to her, much needed in our establishment, decided that we might as well go and live there, and then she
might see a little more of me, and save the travelling-time at least.

It may seem strange to some that a man who has always been
much interested in wild life and nature should be a keen wildfowler
– I actually founded the East Lothian Wildfowlers' Assocation. But I
hold that there is no real conflict. Most wildfowlers are naturalists
too. It is a lonely sport, pursued at dusk and dawn in empty
wind-blown estuaries, with the best sport in the wildest weather
and bags meagre indeed, often non-existent. There is much time
spent in waiting for the flighting duck and geese and much opportunity for communing with nature in all its moods.

There did come a clash, however, between wildfowling and
ornithology, unfortunately when, in 1952 it was decided to turn
Aberlady Bay into Scotland's first Local Nature Reserve, under the
National Parks and Access to the Countryside Act 1947, an English
Act which, typically, had a clause stuck on at the end, as afterthought – this Act shall also apply to Scotland. Not the only one
such, by any means, to cause trouble, when the law of Scotland is

quite distinct from that of England. I protested and persuaded others to protest – and made not a few enemies. Not against the establishment of the nature reserve as such, but because the bye-laws said – thou shalt not shoot ducks and geese. Now, in Scotland, the foreshore, the land between high and low water-mark, is public property, under the *regalia majora* – that is, held in trust for the public by the Crown; whereas in England it is Crown property. The Scots have the public right to access and recreation on the foreshore. Wildfowling, from time immemorial had been an accepted if uncomfortable form of recreation. So the battle was on.

I shall spare you all the arguments, the histrionics and thunder-ings, the defiance, the police warnings and chases out on the dark saltings, the pressmen cursing in the mud, flash-bulbs popping, until at last we were charged, three of us, with breaking the bye-law – which is what we wanted, to get the issue brought to court. We had taken counsel's opinion, and were confident that we would win. And we did. The sheriff found for us, in Scots law – and great were the repercussions and breast-beating. But that was not the end, for of all things, the *Crown* appealed against the findings of its own judge, and on the grounds that the expressed will of the High Court of Parliament at Westminster (the afterthought about the Act also applying to Scotland) was superior to the law of Scotland – the provisions of the Treaty of Union of 1707 notwithstanding. Three ex-politician law lords overturned the sheriff's decision, and the bye-laws stood sacrosanct. However, there was another twist. The Secretary of State for Scotland, who had to confirm the bye-laws, no doubt feeling uncomfortable, added a clause to the effect that duck could continue to be shot but only by permit granted by the Nature Reserve Committee. So I joined the Committee, and helped issue the permits for many a year. Before it all, only perhaps half-a-dozen regulars used to shoot in the bay. Now we issue twenty-five permits annually. Remarkable are the ways of our legislators.

I no longer shoot ducks and geese, but I still walk round Aberlady Bay, and on far beyond, every day, summer and winter; for this is

Aberlady Bay is a great place for wildfowl

the way I write my novels, on the hoof as it were, my peculiar mind seeming to tick over much more productively whilst walking. Scores of novels have been written along this delectable coastline, over the years. My May, bless her, now lies – or what is mortal of her does, although the vital part of her is much more active elsewhere, I am entirely satisfied – in the old kirkyard of Aberlady with its lovely views over that bay, beside Philip our only son – where I hope to join them one day. And the wild-geese skeins still flight over our house, night and morning, calling their strange wild message of freedom, which May loved.

Far beyond the bar of Aberlady Bay, across the silver waters of the Firth of Forth, lies Fife, that independent-minded and most individual peninsula which is another of my favourite places. I have been going to Fife all my life. In my childhood the name was synonymous with holidays, with excitements and long happy days in which the sun always seemed to shine. That was the East Neuk of Fife, the green, golden-lined tip of the long peninsula which thrusts out into the North Sea, with its string of characterful fishing-villages and havens-cum-holiday-resorts – Largo, Elie, St. Monans, Pittenweem, Anstruther, Crail and the rest; but resorts in no sense like the image apt to be conjured up by that term today, just old-world communities which open their doors to discerning summer visitors who rejoice in the leisurely ease and atmosphere to be experienced there, the sandy beaches, the cliffs and coves, the sea-fishing and the walks. Those who seek the swings and round-abouts must go elsewhere.

It was in Elie and Crail that my family used to take houses in July and August; and to Elie that I took May courting, inevitably, since to me it was the equivalent of delight. Indeed, owing to my mother's last illness, our honeymoon had to be divided into two, the first part near enough to Edinburgh to visit her in hospital – so Elie it was again, although we went more adventurously later. Not that we felt in the least deprived in Fife. For one thing, Fife was full of small castles and these were always my joy. Mind you, I would not want it assumed that I chose my honeymoon to pursue my hobby; but one

Crail Harbour, Fife

can combine one's joys – and I don't remember May complaining. Probably she already was becoming reconciled to the enthusiasms and oddities of the man she had married, and as with the duck shooting, perceived that she would get where *she* wanted most readily by seeming to go there by my road. At anyrate, my first book

Robert the Bruce's body is buried in Dunfermline Abbey

was published two years later, on castles. *The Fortalices and Early Mansions of Southern Scotland, 1400–1650* – the sort of title which only a twenty-five-year-old author would dare to inflict upon the public.

It is, probably, seldom realised that West Fife, so different from the East Neuk, used to be called Fothrif, and Dunfermline was its 'capital' an ecclesiastical jurisdiction, whilst Fife proper was a feudal fief of the ancient MacDuff Earls of Fife. Fathrick or Fatrick Moor behind Dunfermline seems to be the only relic of the name remaining. I have always had an interest in Fothrif, too. Robert the Bruce always fascinated me and his body is buried in Dunfermline Abbey – although his heart lies at Melrose, of course; and it was at Dunfermline that Malcolm Canmore wed Margaret Atheling, queen and saint, another figure who greatly interests me. I have written novels about them both.

But there was an especial link with Margaret and Fothrif in which I became concerned – and I use the word link advisedly. The Queen, amongst other good works, established the Queen's Ferry across the Forth near here, to enable pilgrims and poor folk to come to her great new shrine, the stone abbey of Dunfermline, the first great Romish establishment – as distinct from the Celtic Church – in Scotland. This ferry continued, although no longer free, down to present times, now a car-ferry. The queues of vehicles waiting for the ferry-boats became longer and longer as traffic increased – for the ferry saved a forty-mile detour by Kincardine and a lot more by Stirling. The need for a bridge at Queensferry, alongside the famous rail-bridge, was evident and clamorous. But government in far-away London would not listen. So, with one or two others, notably the late Sir Andrew Murray, former Lord Provost of Edinburgh, I set up the National Forth Road Bridge Committee, to campaign for this most necessary link in our road-system, not only to Fife but to Perth, Dundee and all the North. It took us four years to gain the day, years of meetings, rallies, letters-to-the-editors, agitations, with not a few dignified toes trampled upon – but eventually the battle was won and the great bridge was built, a magnificent example of modern engineering, at a cost of over £20 millions – although when we started, it was only to be some £3 millions. But more of that major campaign and undertaking later.

There is a most significant area of Scotland which indeed has been vital in the nation's story and which has long appealed to me,

Stirling Castle guarding the Heartland

for various reasons. In the first of my *Queen's Scotland* volumes I called it *The Heartland.* This is that narrow central waist of the land, between Forth and Clyde, between Highlands and Lowlands, largely Stirlingshire but also part of Perth and Dunbarton shires, most of it anciently known as Monteith, the Mounth or watershed of the River Teith, plus the low lands of Forth and Stirling. It is odd that the Forth and its estuary should be so called, for the Teith is the greater river, both in length and volume of water, and the infant Forth should be its tributary. It joins the Forth just west of Stirling. Nowadays the name is used mainly in the Lake of Menteith – which is often foolishly described as the only lake in Scotland. In fact it was known as the Loch of Monteith always until some Victorian cartographer, presumably of English extraction, seems to have changed loch to lake and Mon to Men. Anciently Monteith was one of the early Celtic earldoms, and with Strathearn to the north formed the important Celtic province of Fortrenn.

The reason for this area's supreme importance in history is partly geographical, partly ethnical. Here, at Stirling, was the lowest point at which the Forth could be bridged – prior to modern engineering techniques – and stretching westwards from Stirling Bridge was over twenty miles of all but impassable marshland, five miles and more wide, the flood-bed of the infant Forth, now largely drained and good agricultural land but its western end still a vast bog known as the Flanders Moss. This extended all the way to the high Pass of Aberfoyle and the mountains culminating in Ben Lomond. So, in effect, you crossed from south to north, from Lowlands to Highlands, in this waist of Scotland either by Stirling Brig or not at all – unless by boat. And even at Stirling the bridge was naturally defended to the north by a mile-wide marsh, spanned by a narrow causeway, so that this suburb of modern Stirling is still called Causewayhead. This tidal barrier could hold up great armies, as Malcolm the Third did the famous Dane, King Canute, and William Wallace did the English might at the Battle of Stirling Bridge. This then is where the greatest struggles of Scotland's bloody history have taken place, Stirling or the approaches thereto – Bannockburn, Sauchieburn, the two Falkirks and the rest. Here Scotland's independence and integrity was saved, time and again.

All this inevitably strongly affected the storyteller in me. But there was another aspect. Monteith, although a Celtic earldom, was also the home of the warlike clan of the MacGregors, Clan Alpine, descended from Alpine King of Scots, Kenneth the First's father, of the 9th century. The saga of the contentious, proud and indestruct-ible clan fascinated me, especially the career of its most famous or notorious character, Rob Roy MacGregor. They it was and they alone who knew the secret routes through the watery wilderness of the Flanders Moss – and enthusiastically they made use of the knowledge to raid the Southron's cattle and drive the beasts back to the security of their mountain fastnesses. Rob Roy elaborated this more subtly into a widespread and successful protection racket whereby you either paid the MacGregors your 'mail' – blackmail, if you like – for the protection of your stock and herds, or else you lost them, an early development of the insurance industry. As well as being the master of this trade, Rob Roy was of course a notable leader of the Jacobite cause in guerilla warfare – and I wrote three novels and a children's book on this and related themes.

It was whilst researching 'in the field' for the first book, *Mac-Gregor's Gathering,* that I discovered the sad state of the road westwards of Aberfoyle, which ended at Inversnaid on the shore of Loch Lomond – Rob Roy was MacGregor of Inversnaid. For four miles this lovely coiling road through the birchwoods and moun-tains was almost as impassable as the Flanders Moss, deliberately kept in disrepair by Glasgow city water authority, whose water supply came from the lochs of Katrine and Arklet here. They wanted to discourage visitors, allegedly in the interests of water purity – although all the water had to go through purification filters anyway. This policy resulted in the virtual cutting off of the little community of Inversnaid, which had no other access save by the pier on the loch. The children somehow or other had to be got over this four-mile hazard daily, to the nearest school at Aberfoyle, and serious was the deprivation. So, with my old friend Wilfred Taylor of the *Scotsman* newspaper, renowned writer of *A Scotsman's Log* – who co-operated with me on other ventures – and George Buchan who farmed Inversnaid and with his wife ran the hotel there, we set up the Glen Arklet Road Committee, to fight to get the road rehabilitated. Glasgow Corporation was very annoyed, and I made some more unfriends undoubtedly. But eventually public opinion was mobilised and the city authorities gave way. The road was repaired with good tarmac. Much rejoicing at Inversnaid – where in the hotel we in due course launched *MacGregor's Gathering* in most distinguished company but without any Glasgow councillors – company which included Wilfred Taylor and the *Scotsman's* helpful editor, Alastair M. Dunnett.

Other Heartland ploys there have been, naturally, but that is enough for the present.

In any preliminary survey of my most favoured parts of the country, I could nowise omit the Glen Feshie and Rothiemurchus area of the Central Highlands, in Inverness-shire, which has always spelt enchantment and inspiration for me and mine. This is that most lovely terrain on the north-west side of the Cairngorm Mountains, now 'developed' in the Aviemore and Glen More vicinities thanks – or otherwise – to the snow-corries of Cairngorm for skiing purposes and allied joys. Still, nine-tenths of the area is still unspoiled and at least many more people, prepared to walk, know and explore it than heretofore. I came walking and climbing here from the age of seventeen onwards; here May and I had our second and 'major' honeymoon two months after the first; here our children equated with heaven, and Philip learned the rudiments of what was going to turn him into a noted mountaineer; and here in due course Frances May spent her own honeymoon. Here too was the background and inspiration for my first novel – unpublishable, fortunately, so clever an epic was it – and for the next, *Trespass* and many another.

May loved Rothiemurchus Forest, with its ancient Caledonian pines and rushing dipper-haunted rivers, above all places upon earth. I am writing this there, now, nine months after her death, and feeling her near.

Two more areas must suffice meantime – the vast wonderland of the North West Highlands and Inner Hebrides, and the very different central Aberdeenshire. What can I say about the North-West which has not been said a hundred times before? Nothing, save

The islands of Eigg and Rhum from Moidart

that I personally see it as the most hauntingly beautiful territory on the planet – when the sun shines. And there is so much of it, literally a thousand miles and more of coloured enchanted seaboard, where the names of Calgary, Sunart, Moidart, Knoydart, Kintail, Torridon, Sleat, Edrachillis, Clashnessie, Durness, Scullamy and scores more, sing their siren-song for me. I could be a great bore about the Hebridean Sea and its environs.

Another of my little road campaigns was fought up here – or rather, fought elsewhere, in places where pressure could usefully be brought, but relating to this seaboard. The road along the north shore of Loch Torridon ended at Inveralligin – and very nice too.

But beyond Inveralligin some six miles, over a high saddle and down into a deep, hidden hollow, is Loch Diabaig and its crofting township. Only a rough, unmetalled dirt-track led to this dramatically attractive place. The little community was dying for want of access – as so many others have died in our beautiful Highlands, where young folk will not stay for want of some simple amenity. There had been fifty occupied houses, with their crofts, not long before, at Diabaig; but by 1956 there were only sixteen left. So the Torridon and Red Point Road Committee was established, again Wilfred Taylor, and Kenneth Macpherson, the keeper of the one little shop, and myself taking the initiative. We attracted quite a lot of support for this one, with a public meeting there attended by the local M.P. and other notables. This got the road to Diabaig built by the West Ross authorities more speedily than we might have expected, more sympathetic once the need was pushed under their good noses. But we did not get the road carried on to Red Point, as we had hoped. The one to Diabaig was quite tricky to build, too, with startling gradients.

A lot further south, in Lorn, my one and only film was made, in 1958 – *Bridal Path*. I have had many film options taken on my books, but this is the only one, so far, to reach celluloid. It was about a Hebridean islander who came to the mainland here in search of a bride, a simple tale. Many will have seen it, with Bill Travers starring, for it gets repeated on TV occasionally. It was shot on location in the Oban, Easdale, Appin and Barcaldine areas, and we had much fun in the process, taking part in crowd scenes. I remember well getting my head in my hands from wife and children for not allowing them to queue up for the small fees for extras, as being unsuitable in the author's family.

There was a sequel to this film-making. For when it came to holding the required formal premiere, I managed to insist that this should be held, not in London as the producers had intended, but in Edinburgh. And a great occasion it proved to be, the first World Premiere of a motion picture held in Scotland, with a high-powered social jamboree at the New Victoria Cinema (now the Odeon) with large amounts of money being paid for seats, to the benefit of two charities I selected, the Royal Scottish Society for the Prevention of Cruelty to Children and the Scottish National Institution for the War Blinded. It was attended by the stars Bill Travers, Virginia McKenna and Fiona Clyne, and many who were scarcely stars then but who became famous later on, such as Duncan Macrae, Roddy Macmillan, George Cole, Gordon Jackson, Terry Scott, Jameson Clark, and of course the director and producer, Frank Launder and Sidney Gilliat. Edinburgh society made a night of it, with dukes, marquesses, and judges glad to be seen at the pictures. Considering how simple a story it was all based on, it is perhaps surprising how successful the picture became. It went down particularly well, strange to say, in Russia, was drooled over somewhat embarrassingly in America, and was the Queen's choice at Balmoral for Princess Margaret's 29th birthday evening.

I shall wind up this preliminary survey with one favourite which we came to know and appreciate late in life. I knew Deeside, of course, and something of Donside and the vicinity of Aberdeen itself. But I had no idea as to the size, variety and attractiveness of the vast hinterland until I came to write the *Queen's Scotland* volume on the area. A glance at the map will reveal that this is indeed the greatest slab of sheer country in all Scotland. I read somewhere that there were ten thousand farms in Aberdeenshire, and took this as something of a flourish of the pen. Now I know better. I would say that it is a major underestimate. Here is a land again quite distinct from the rest, little visited save by those with reason to go there, over two thousand square miles of it, of low green hills, great rivers, winding side-roads, far vistas and cattle-strewn pastureland everywhere. More beef must come from Aberdeenshire than from any similar area of these islands. It is not exciting country like others I have described but it has immense character, a settled, rural and quite populous land, well-doing, prosperous, but the reverse of soft. The farms are not large, like those of Lothian or Galloway, their sturdy, grey-granite houses modest but strong, adequate – like the folk. The towns are small and neatly functional and have all been there a long time. One can go on exploring Aberdeenshire and never quite come to the end of it – nor want to. And there are more castles remaining to the square mile than anywhere else in the land. Whether North Sea oil will adversely affect this fine countryside remains to be seen – probably not in any serious way, since it is so extensive. But at least the money and the entrepreneurish folk it has brought to Aberdeen and Peterhead and the rest has helped in the restoration of some of its many ruined castles – which is a bonus dear to my heart.

These examples which I have chosen *are* only examples. So many more I could extol and acclaim, each with its own special attraction for myself as for others. But enough is enough.

chapter two
THE PEOPLE

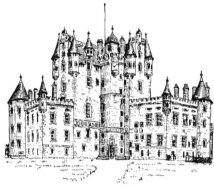

As I have suggested, the Scots people are by no means all that their popular image – or their own self-esteem – would have the world believe. And is there such a thing as a typical Scot? I doubt it. To understand this and to perceive some of the reasons, I suggest that it is necessary to know something of the story of the race – which is, of course, history. Far be it from me, here, to go deeply into the origins of the species or its troubled tale. But a page or two might be readily digested and helpful.

The modern Scot, of course, is no more 'pure' racially than any other nation today. There have been constant admixtures down the ages – Norsemen, Angles, Saxons, Normans, Irish, and to be sure, latterly, English, of the 'executive' class. But the basic stock, which except in specific pockets has absorbed all these, remains. And that basic stock is, I assert, in the main Pictish – however many eyebrows may be raised at this, even by the said Pictish descendants. Before you dismiss me as some sort of blinkered antiquarian, read on.

The Picts were the first known inhabitants of this land, a Celtic people who came originally from that cradle of races, the Middle

East, probably via Ireland. That name was only given them by the Roman invaders, and almost certainly referred to the people who communicated in pictures, rather than caligraphy – certainly not the ridiculous story that they were barbarians who painted their bodies blue; they would not have needed to do this, for anyone who went more or less naked in our climate would have been blue already and come to swift extinction. Their true Celtic name was the Cruithne. Now, the nearest Gaelic word to cruithne is *cruithneachd* which means wheat. I suggest that they were so-called as a wheat-growing people, at a time when most men were hunters. At anyrate, they were a cultured folk, as their pictures still reveal, graphically carved on their famous symbol-stones and crosses.

*Pictish
Symbol Stone,
9–10th century*

These tell us what clothing they wore, the armour and weapons they used, that they were great hunters on horseback and with hounds, that their priestly caste, for sun-worship, was highly important with elaborate vestments, that they had major engineering skills and that they were artistic to a marked degree, their designs intricate and imaginative. And so on.

The Picts occupied not only Alba – the land north of the Forth and Clyde, which was their main heartland, with its capital at Inverness – but southern Scotland also and quite a long way down into England, even as far as Yorkshire it is believed. This might account for much! Queen Elizabeth Tudor's name for Hadrian's Wall in Northumbria was the Pecht's Wall. For how many centuries the Picts had the land to themselves, we do not know. But in the fifth century, Fergus MacErc, King of Dalriada in Antrim, crossed the Irish Sea with his brothers and supporters and settled in what we now call Argyll, which he renamed Dalriada after his homeland. These were the Scots. There is a picturesque tradition that they

took this name from Scota, an Egyptian princess who eloped with a Celtic princeling and fled to Ireland taking with her the semi-magic *Lia Fail,* later called the Stone of Destiny, alleged to be Jacob's pillow in the Bible story. I would not place entire credence on that, but these legends usually have some basis, and it may well be merely the old Middle East Celtic origin surfacing again.

So the Scots had come to Alba, and set up a colony, but in very small numbers. Presumably the Picts accepted them, did not treat them as invaders – after all, they were fellow-Celts – for they could have driven the colonists out of Dalriada quite easily, but did not do so. No doubt the Scots intermarried with the Pictish women from an early stage.

Then a century later came Columba, also of royal Irish blood, bearing the Christian message and fleeing from trouble in Ireland. He and his followers settled at Iona, off the Dalriadic coast, and from there proceeded indefatigably to convert first his fellow-Scots and then the Picts. Further and further he spread the Gospel,

Iona –
the restored Abbey

Stone Circle – Ring of Brogar, Orkney

using much of the native sun-worship symbolism to make things easier for his converts, a sensible and broad-minded attitude however frowned upon by the Romish Church – for Columba was essentially a practical man. The Scots word kirk can be derived from circle, the stone-circles of the sun-worshippers; and many of the Columban cells and churches were established within these circles. Some old Aberdeenshire parish churches are still so-placed.

Columba went all over Alba, apparently accepted by the Picts; and at Inverness converted Brude, the High King himself. So Pic-

policy of introducing foreigners, largely to staff the new Romish Church which she was so determined must replace the Celtic or Columban Church, which she, a devout Catholic, considered to be heretical. Three of her sons became Kings of Scots in succession; and David, the youngest, having been taken, as hostage for his brothers' good behaviour, to the Norman Court at Winchester, grew up in England and made his friends amongst the young Normans. When he finally ascended the throne, he brought a large number of these with him, and kept importing more, in his great design of turning Scotland from a patriarchal Celtic nation into a feudal and, for that period, modern state, organised in shires, parishes and dioceses. Thus to Scotland came the Stewarts, Frasers, Lindsays, Bruces, Comyns or Cummings, Gordons, Chisholms and a host more, names which are now accepted as Scots. These young Normans made a policy of marrying Scots heiresses, to gain lands and estates, as the Scots from Dalriada had done before them.

This process was never repeated on any large scale, however. There were other influxes of foreigners, notably Flemings from the Low Countries; but these were mainly merchants, traders and artisans, imported to establish specific industries and commerce. Some became rich and married into the aristocracy – the Flemings, Earls of Wigtown and Lords of Cumbernauld for instance; but as a rule these immigrants were absorbed into the general population. Later, in the time of the Regent, Mary of Guise, widow of James the Fifth, and of Mary Queen of Scots her daughter, there was a sizeable infusion of French blood, these queens bringing in many artists, poets, secretaries, architects and soldiers as well as courtiers. But though these made a large impact on Scottish culture, especially in castle-building, and on the language, catering and music, they had no great effect on the ethnic situation. It was not until the Industrial Revolution period that there was any new major infusion of blood, when the need for cheap labour, coinciding with the Irish famines, brought large numbers of Irish, mainly to Glasgow and the industrial south-west. These, of course, were also of Celtic extraction; but their impact was quite pronounced and even divisive at times,

Midmar Castle, Aberdeenshire.
An excellent example of late 16th century fortified house

largely for two reasons – they were nearly all Roman Catholic whilst Scotland was by now staunchly Protestant in the main; and they were poor, peasantry, who came because they were starving, and they tended to remain poor and be kept that way in the new industrial society, producing what became known as the Glasgow – Irish problem – which has not entirely disappeared, even today.

There has, in more recent years, been one other admixture – that of the English-born folk who have come to Scotland in growing numbers, for a variety of reasons – as civil servants and other minions of London government; as chiefs of branch offices and factories and so on; as academics in our universities; as so-called white settlers in the Highlands; and as folk opting out of the rat-race in the South. The effect of these 'executive' immigrants has been more pronounced in some areas than others, for naturally they tend to congregate in the 'better social' areas. This county of mine, East Lothian, for instance, being conveniently close to Edinburgh the capital, is much affected. Many of these good folk become very fond of Scotland and the Scots and say they would not go back to England for anything. Not a few even join the Scottish National Party!

That, then, is our racial background – and presumably has some responsibility for the odd kind of people we are – that, and the religious influence, which has had a lot to do with our development. I have evolved a theory about this, which is possibly quite erronious but which seems to me to fit the case. I suggest that the practical, moderate, 'democratic' sort of Christianity of the early Celtic Church, which evolved more or less naturally out of Columba's missionary endeavours, was good for us, suited to the Scottish temperament – and should have been left to develop more or less normally. Instead, the well-meaning Margaret and her sons imposed the hierarchial Romish faith upon the country, with its strict dogma and disciplines, its ranks of archbishop, bishop, abbot, prior and the rest, its elaborate ritual and its subservience to the Pope in Rome. I am not saying that these were not, in their way, good in themselves – or some of them – but that they were foreign to the Scots character and traditions, Mediterranean Christianity in fact, more suited to the demonstrative people of the south than to ourselves. It is just possible that there would never have been the need for a dire and drastic Reformation in Scotland if the old Celtic Church had been allowed to remain. It had grown decadent, to be sure – but so had the Romish one, so have all

John Knox's House, Edinburgh – doubtful Knox
but authentic vernacular architecture

branches of Christianity from time to time, and been renewed and reformed from within; the Benedictines, the Tironensians, the Vallescaulians and many other Roman reforming influences testify to that. When the Reformation did come to Scotland, of course, it was the more wholesale, sweeping, tending to throw out the baby with the bath-water, and almost as alien to the Scots character as what it replaced. The harsh and stern, extreme and unsmiling type of Calvinism which then took over was by no means natural to us – but for centuries was vehemently imposed, and still persists in some measure in some parts. The religious wars of the seventeenth century were not between Protestants and Catholics but between two forms of Protestantism – with, to be sure, political and dynastic overtones.

So the Scots, basically a religious race in the sense of being much concerned with metaphysics and the unseen, but in a relaxed way, have been constrained and pressed into moulds which by no means suited their natural tendencies. This, I am convinced, has made them the more disputatious and thrawn.

We have, I suppose, so far been looking on the less admirable side of the canvas. There is the other aspect, the more positive side of our nature, which has made the Scots one of the most adventurous of races, with great initiative and powers of leadership – indeed has made them leaders all over the world, outside their own country, where oddly enough they are in the mass so argumentative as never to unite on any issue and so allow others to take over the lead. In other words, they are a race of individualists. They are, at base, hard-working, reliable, ambitious, self-reliant, courageous, inventive and with a great respect for knowledge and education. They are romantics by nature, but have sought to hide this under a cloak of gruff, down-to-earth, plain-speaking and pretended realism – the Calvinist influence, almost certainly. A complex folk by any standards.

It is necessary, I agree, to differentiate in some measure between the Highland and Lowland character – but not so much as some have suggested; for as has been shown, we are all the same basic

Black-house, reed-thatched, on Mull

strain, although undoubtedly there has been more non-Celtic admixture in the Lowlands. But for some centuries the two group-ings remained very much apart, for historical and geographical reasons, and tended to develop differently and with markedly dissimilar outlooks on many things. The Normanising, feudalising influence never spread effectively beyond the Highland Line, where the patriarchial or clan system continued to flourish long after it was replaced in the Lowlands. Likewise the Reformation made only a modest impact in the North-West. So that the Highlan-ders, until the Jacobite period and the dire upheavals thereafter, were allowed to remain with fewer pressures on them. As a result they developed in more naturally Celtic fashion presumably, more easy-going, less assertive, some would say more lazy, although less *driven* might be more accurate. Nowadays of course, what with the deliberate governmental policy of ending the clan-system and using up the manpower in the army and imperial expansion, with the Clearances emptying the glens and emigration encouraged, the Highlands are largely depopulated, with only one-twentieth of the five million people living there – and a far from negligible proportion of these incomers -- something of a problem area, more and more given over to tourism, recreation and the catering therefor, and forestry. But the influx of Highland folk into Lowland Scotland, especially into the Glasgow area where, like the Irish cheap labour, immigrants also flocked, has had its effect on the character of the rest. This double infusion, in the first half of the nineteenth century, goes a long way to explain the very different attitudes and behaviour of Edinburgh and Glasgow people, something which has long mystified visitors, considering that the two great cities are only forty miles apart.

A word or two must be said about the Scots abroad – and according to some assessments there are twenty million of them, although this may be an exaggeration. Anyway, there are undoubtedly many more than in Scotland. In these, the effects of environment and external pressures – or lack of them – can be seen most vividly. For these, by and large, have developed into a markedly different sub-species. Whilst retaining a strong sense of their Scots nationality and a profound and sometimes almost maudlin romantic concern for everything Scottish, they have almost everywhere, in Canada, the United States, New Zealand, Australia, the African countries and elsewhere, done notably well for themselves, risen to positions of eminence, power and leadership, marking themselves out as a rather especial people. To the fourth and fifth generations of the original emigrants they delight in keeping the old traditions alive – there are many more Gaelic-speakers outside than within Scotland – holding clan-gatherings, forming St. Andrew and Caledonian societies, Scots dancing-clubs and so on. Some of these activities and over-enthusiastic and nostalgic ongoings would cause Scots at home to raise their more carefully controlled eyebrows, admittedly – but then, when these overseas Scots make their inevitable pilgrimages back to the old country, they too tend to raise eyebrows at what they see here and shake heads into the bargain. They may well have the rights of it.

I apologise if I have gone on over-long about the Scots people and their character and characteristics – but as a novelist I have to be intensely interested in character and what makes folk tick the way they do. For those concerned for Scotland and the Scots it is surely important to recognise why they are *different*. That they are not better than other people is self-evident, despite the assertions of the 'here's tae us, wha's like us!' school of ignoramuses; but they *are* different. *Vive la difference!* It will be a sorrier world when we are all the same, as the bureaucrats would like.

Let me end this by recounting what really first caused me to recognise and consider this difference between Scots and others, in a deliberate way. It was in the army when, after being commissioned into an artillery regiment I found myself appointed Welfare Officer, amongst other duties. One of my tasks was to read and censor all letters written by the troops – something I much objected to doing, in principle, but required by higher authority in the interests of security. By that stage in the war the regiment had become a very mixed lot indeed, with replacements and reinforcements from almost everywhere under the sun; and the men's letter-writing was most revealing, however deplorable the need to scan it. We had a proportion of Scots in the unit, perhaps one in fifteen, and some rough customers amongst them. But what intrigued me was that, without looking at addresses or names, I could pick out the Scots letters immediately I began to read. The handwriting might be poor but the vocabulary was always much wider, the expression of feeling less hackneyed, imagination given more scope, the whole thing more fluent – even though the spelling was not always immaculate. And this from tough characters who would have blushed to the roots of their hair to have to speak aloud these sentiments and phrases, and who, on the face of it, were much less eloquent than their English, Welsh, Irish and other fellow-soldiers – or perhaps I should substitute glib for eloquent? I moved to other units, later in the war and found the same thing, and it set me thinking.

I have been thinking about it, off and on, ever since.

chapter three
INTERACTION

So there we have the land and the people. Perhaps it is worth looking briefly at how land and people have interacted, the pressures one on the other, and how together they have joined to maintain Scotland as an entity down the eventful centuries – for surely never has a land, the actual countryside, contributed more to the defence and independence of a nation than has Scotland – even though, in return, the Scots have grievously neglected and misused the said land.

The assault, of course, for seven hundred years, was always from England, determined and continuous; and every one of Scotland's leaders, who directed the marathon struggle, used the land strategically to help him – for it so happened that this land was notably apt for defensive warfare under skilled hands. I shall not try to detail that prolonged struggle here; but it is helpful for any understanding of land and people to recognise something of what was, until the 18th century – and in a different way since then also, perhaps – the over-riding preoccupation of the Scots, other than religious hair-splitting – the maintaining of a national identity and freedom from external domination and absorption.

Such contemplation implies no hatred of the English nor of England – far from it. Personally I have an enormous admiration and affection for that people, their qualities of determination and assurance, their totally unconscious nationalism, sense of unity, unconcern with the whys as distinct from the hows – and their sublime conviction that they are God's favourite creation – many of which qualities the Scots lack grievously. I have English forebears myself, and by no means deplore the fact, although I look upon myself as a Scot.

Why were the English so consistent in their efforts to dominate the Scots, generation after generation? It was far more than a mere case of territorial aggression and empire-building, although it started that way. It could not have been because of fear of a reverse domination, with the vast English superiority in numbers. Some knowledge of the historical background supplies us with at least some of the answers. It seems to have started in the 11th century with religious rather than military or political pressures, or at least Church politics rather than civil ones – this before Margaret and her efforts to Romanise the Celtic Church. Because of this Columban Church and its non-hierarchical system and lack of central authority, there were no archbishops or metropolitans of the Papal faith north of York. The fact that there were no episcopal dioceses either did not concern the Romish prelates. They reached the conclusion that, under the Pope, Christ's Vicar, these lands to the north must *have* a metropolitan, at least in name – and it could be only themselves at York, or the Norse Archbishop of Nidaros, which of course was unthinkable. So, they assumed spiritual hegemony over the heretical Scots, if without being able to do anything about it. Probably it sounded well in Rome. Then King Canute, an ambitious Dane, who had assumed the newly-united English throne and called himself Emperor of the Anglo-Saxons and Danes, discovered this Yorkist religious hegemony theory and saw its use towards extending his own new empire. Malcolm the Second had to cope, not very adequately, with the results. King MacBeth, a little later, was more successful in rejecting such spiritual arrogance; but when his successor and slayer, Malcolm Canmore, found himself faced with that formidable Norman, William the Conqueror, using the same Yorkist aspirations for his own further efforts at conquering, he was less fortunate, certainly less far-seeing. Malcolm, not a bright character, to get rid of William from Scots soil, went through to him a meaningless ceremony of making fealty to William for the land, a feudal concept which had no relevance to the Celtic idea of thrones or land-tenure. But thereafter, one after another, the Kings of England claimed that the Kings of Scots were sub-kings to themselves, vassals, and that *they* were Lords Paramount of Scotland; whilst the Archbishops of York claimed spiritual dominance more strongly than ever, since Malcolm's wife and sons had now turned Scotland officially Roman Catholic. It was not until an anti-English Pope was persuaded to promote the senior Catholic bishop of Scotland, St. Andrew, to be an archbishop and metropolitan, that this spiritual overlordship nonsense finally collapsed. But by that time the English kings had it firmly fixed as a priority that Scotland should pay them feudal homage. This continued right up to the time of Henry the Eighth, who tried very hard, in what became known as the Rough Wooing, to take over Scotland, first by force of arms and then by marriage. His daughter, Elizabeth Tudor does not seem to have done anything much about it, except intrigue, having her eyes fixed much further afield. Then, of course, Scots James the Sixth ascended the English throne, uniting the two kingdoms although not the nations – and the long monarchical tussle was terminated, and in the opposite way from all English aspirations.

In this long-continued struggle against English domination, the land played almost as important a part as did the people. When it came to defensive warfare Scotland was hard to beat, a land cut up by great estuaries and innumerable sea-lochs, of rushing rivers and endless hills, of cliffs and rocks and woods, of narrow gorges and passes, and above all, of marsh and bog, undrained swampy land in which heavy cavalry, the English principal weapon from Norman times, was useless. Always the Scots aim was to lure the

massive hosts of armoured knights, mounted on their great de-
striers, into soft ground which would not bear their weight, to
entangle the dreaded archers in close woodland and scrub where
they had no field-of-fire, to coax the ranks of foot into the hills
where they could be ambushed, strung out thinly in narrow passes,
to force enemy attacks across rushing rivers and, when outnum-
bered hopelessly or out-manoeuvred, to have lochs and estuaries
to retire behind. Thus fought MacBeth and Wallace and Bruce, the
Black Douglas, James the Fourth and the great Montrose. Despite
all the might so consistently marshalled against them – and the
shameful internal wrangling within, for Scotland has never lacked
those who would rather betray their fellows than their theories and
even their pockets – the land was never conquered.

These many centuries of the threat of English assault and domination have inevitably left their mark on the Scots people even
today, often in a wary, touchy attitude not exactly hostile but
prepared to be so, a grudging, critical chip-on-the-shoulder outlook which is rather sad, really.

So much for the land and people's co-operation in defence. What
of the other side, in production and cherishing? Here the picture is
more confused, with major variations. In my East Lothian, for
instance, where is some of the best agricultural land in the United
Kingdom, it is also amongst the best-farmed and managed; it has to
be, to pay the enormous rents. This has resulted in many of the old
land-owning families being able to hang on to their estates as in
few other parts of these islands. East Lothian was the cradle of the
land-improvement movement, where many of the great names and
experimenters and innovators in that important art or science
have originated and operated – Cockburn of Ormiston, Fletcher of
Saltoun, Meikle, Wight, Hope and the rest. Nowhere have such
yields, especially in barley and potatoes, been surpassed.

On the other hand, it is safe to say that in few parts of Europe has
the land been so grossly neglected and ill-used as in the Highlands
of Scotland. I have taken Danish visitors there, who have been
shocked at what they saw – the Danes of course being meticulous

Lowland farmland, agricultural excellence, with panorama of East Lothian

to cultivate every available inch of their land. The reason for this is two-fold, ancient and more modern. There was never any tradition of intensive cultivation in the Highlands; and admittedly a mountainous terrain is difficult and less than rewarding agriculturally. Nevertheless there were and are large areas everywhere which *could* be cultivated and are not. In the old clan days the economy was sustained on cattle, and cultivation was more or less restricted to growing winter-feed for the beasts, plus some oats for the pot and griddle. Indeed working the land was considered no suitable toil for a man of spirit and was largely left to the women, whilst the menfolk herded, fished, hunted, fought and discussed higher things. Still, since there was quite a large population to sustain, a considerable amount of land was tilled, if less than intensively.

But then, with the unsuccessful Jacobite Risings of 1715 and 1745, and London government's alarmed decision to destroy the clan system once and for all, the scene changed entirely. The glens were partly cleared and fierce repression prevailed. Then hot on the heels of this came the Napoleonic Wars and Britain under blockade. Growing all our own food became vital – but scarcely so in the Highlands, which the authorities in the south decided would conveniently make vast sheep-runs – despite the fact that it had always been cattle, not sheep, which had been the support of the people there, and sheep are selective grazers and not good for the land. So the glens were forcibly emptied of the folk, in the notorious Clearances, and the former clansmen driven to eke out a miserable existence on the barren shoreline or else to emigrate to the Lowland cities or overseas; and North Country English shepherds imported to run the huge hirsels. At the same time, the Highlanders were being formed into innumerable Highland regiments by the former chiefs, to go fight Napoleon, as a way by which these ex-Jacobite leaders could win their way back into government favour. So the Highlands were denuded, a grim chapter in Scotland's story.

This state of affairs continued until the Victorian era when, thanks largely to the Queen's own example and embracing of a sort of romantic balmorality, it became the thing for the rich, and especially the great new class of prosperous manufacturers thrown up by the Industrial Revolution, to own a grouse-moor or deer-forest in the Highlands of Scotland. Shooting-lodges went up by the hundred in the glens and straths, the kilt, banned after the Forty-five as seditious, came back, largely on English Midland shanks, and for some six weeks in the year the Highlands were populated again, by the sportsmen, their families and guests and hordes of servants. But sheep do not go well with grouse and spoil the deer-stalking – so the sheep had to go, after a reign of a mere

Balmorality – Queen Victoria's gesture towards Highland romanticism

Highland pastoral scene – tilled land non-existent

half-century or so. The land itself remained neglected of course, for shooting gentry required no crops – nor did the gamekeepers and stalkers, who became the new resident autocrats of the Highlands. Only in the far North-West and the Hebrides did the indigenous crofters manage to cling on, where indeed the soil was poorest.

So we come down to this century, when three new elements have affected the picture – forestry, hydro-electrics and tourism. The first two have certainly made an impact on the land, but scarcely in a fashion to cheer the Scots. The Forestry Commission is now the

Highland forestry, decently diversified, with artificial hydro-electric Loch Faskally

greatest landowner in Scotland, with well over a million acres planted, and the serried, close-order ranks of conifers march over endless miles of the Highland scene. Far be it from me to declare that this is a bad thing in its entirety. We in these islands badly need to grow our own timber to save vast imports, and the Highlands grow timber well – after all, once they were pretty well covered by the ancient Caledonian Forest. Also forestry brings people, a few, to the empty glens, although once the ploughing and planting is over, it is one of the least labour-intensive of industries. Small forestry communities have sprung up here and there, and even little Highland schools which had been closed have re-opened, to deal with the foresters' children. This is to the good. Also the Commission is now adopting a more helpful attitude, encouraging visitors to its vast territories, laying out forest-walks and information-centres and beginning to diversify the single-tree-species policy. But there is another side to it all. Forestry is putting paid, for ever, to any hope of a revival of the *people's* land-use in the Highland area, to the old pasture-and-crop systems – for those tree-stumps and roots, even if all were cut down, will never now be grubbed out. Much land suitable for secondary agriculture has been planted and though legislation was introduced belatedly prohibiting the Commission from planting arable, this did not do much good, for no Highland farmer or crofter can make a living out of such arable alone; and if the rough pasture of the surrounding hillsides is planted, as it is, then the little oases of arable scattered in the valley-floors are of no use to anyone, hidden away amongst the forests. Soon these grow over with natural self-planted seed-lings.

If the Highlands represented a less important proportion of the entire Scottish land-total, all this might be the less serious.

The hydro-electric threat to the land is for the present largely dormant – although with the fuel-famine hitting the western world ever more direly, who knows when it may start up again? But in the 1950s this was a serious matter for the Highlands. Again I do not say that it was altogether deleterious; the country needed electricity and the Highland lochs and rivers could produce water-power in a huge way – even if most of the current generated was said to be going to England. But the trouble was, of course, that the necessary dams and reservoirs had to be constructed in the valleys, and innumerable valley-floors were flooded. And that was where the arable was. So again the land, as such, suffered. Farms were swept away, small communities disappeared – and fortunes were made by land-speculators. I wrote a novel about this, called *The Chosen Course* – and for a while after publication was somewhat

Hydro-electric dam and fish-ladder, Loch Faskally, Pitlochry

apprehensive lest a certain millionaire contractor involved in the lucrative business of finding out where hydro-electric developments were likely to take place, buying the land cheap and selling dear thereafter, should esteem himself libelled by my story. Probably he never read novels and I need not have been concerned.

I did more than just write fiction about all this, however. The

Clan Albainn Society was founded in 1948, largely by ex-Servicemen who had come home with opened eyes as to what was happening to Scotland, and a desire to do something about it. I became first its Edinburgh branch chairman and then, for a year, the national chairman. Its objects were to settle men and their families on crofting and farming land in the Highlands which had gone back to the wilderness – and first of all, of course, to acquire such land. I must say that we had a hard row to hoe, for land-owners, whether private or corporate, and certainly governmental, were not interested and of course we had no large funds at our disposal. But there were plenty of eager settlers anxious to start anew on the outdoor life. We did find one large landowner, in Wester Ross, who was prepared to give us a trial, at least. We settled our first group of six pioneers on the Scoraig peninsula, in the Loch Broom area, on disused crofting land. All went well at first, with the settlers preparing the ground, stone-clearing and planting. Others queued up to be allowed to join them, if we could get more land. So passed the first spring and summer, when the men, even families, could live in tents. But more substantial accommodation was required for the winter; and it was at this stage that we ran into trouble – and with, of all things, the Crofters' Acts legislation. It transpired that should any settler or tenant of crofting land decide to leave after a few years, the landowner would be liable under this legislation to pay quite substantial compensation. No landowner was likely to hail this with enthusiasm. In vain we protested that this was not, repeat not, the Society's policy; and we sought to get Lloyds to insure us against any such risk, for the benefit of the landowner, but they would not touch it. It was the need to rebuild croft-houses which brought it to a head. We tried hard to get the politicians to do something about it, and I wrote at the time to point out that Scotland was being bombarded by a multiplicity of organisations, official and other-wise, beseeching the Scots young folk to go abroad, to the empty places overseas – and pointing out that Scotland had her own empty places which should come first. I called upon the Secretary of State and government to implement their powers under the Land Settlement Acts – but governmental interest was nil. So the Crofters' Acts, deliberately designed to help in land-settlement, were working right against us, and it was the business of nobody in authority to try to put the matter right. The whole scheme foundered, amidst recriminations from within and without. I resigned, to make way for a new chairman and a new start – but this came to nothing. Not one of my most successful ventures – although personally I learned a lot.

I wrote a novel called *The Freebooters,* to dramatise the situation, not only of land-settlement and use but of dealing with all the frustrations and thou-shalt-not restrictions and artificial shortages of those post-war years in Scotland. It sold very well and was serialised in the national press – so possibly more folk had the situation brought to their notice, certainly outwith Scotland, than ever heard of the Clan Albainn Society. Whether it did any good is an open question. It is interesting, reading over that novel today after the lapse of time, to perceive how little further forward we are in the early 1980s.

In these last two decades tourism, as an organised industry, has hit the Highlands in especial; and once again, whether for good or ill is a moot point. Probably it was inevitable, given the magnificent scenery and the great increase in personal mobility and leisure. But it does tend to alter things, in a country of small population; not so much the land as the people. Catering for the tourist has become a preoccupation, which does not necessarily bring out the best in us; and much that is authentic and simple seems to get swept away in the flood. One thing is certain, it does not *help* the land. The bed-and-breakfast notices proliferate – and no harm in that; we found these facilities most useful when we were doing the *Queen's Scotland* books, with much kindness thrown in. But not an extra acre gets cultivated – the reverse probably true, as catering becomes the more important and profitable.

I am sorry about the land which in all honesty I can say that I love. We do not deserve it, any of us.

chapter four
GOVERNMENT AND MISGOVERNMENT

Ploughing through all this, one aspect of it all must surely strike even the most casual reader – the self-evident fact that Scotland is not well governed and has not been for a long time. One does not require to be any sort of nationalist nor student of political theory to perceive this; it shouts aloud in Scotland's story. This is strange, considering how high in the art and practice of government the Scots have risen, outwith their own land. Just think, for instance of the number of Scots Prime Ministers of the United Kingdom within the last hundred years or so – Gladstone, Roseberry, Balfour, Campbell-Bannerman, Bonar Law, Ramsay Macdonald, Macmillan, Douglas-Home; to say nothing of those of Scottish extraction who have reached similar heights in the Dominions and former colonies. Yet here, at home, there has been most evidently a continuing failure to manage and develop the land for the benefits of its people in practically every walk of life which government affects – and today central government affects practically everything.

It would be easy to declare, as many do, that it all stems from absentee government, from rule from London since 1707, when Scotland lost her own parliament under the Treaty of Union,

Old Parliament Hall, Edinburgh – now an adjunct of the Law Courts

pushed through in most shameful and disreputable fashion and against the will of the great mass of the Scots people. But undoubtedly there is more to it than that. If the Scots, as a whole, had urgently desired and demanded the right to govern themselves again, they could have achieved this time and again during the intervening nearly three centuries – but did not, even though it has been a near thing once or twice. Why? The Irish did, bloodily, and every sizeable part of the old Empire did, one way and another, many with smaller and less 'national' populations than Scotland.

It seems to me that we must look for the reasons for this towards something in the Scots people themselves, in their character and attitudes. I have, indeed, already indicated that I see the answer to many of our corporate failures – as distinct from our personal and individual successes – in the extraordinary divisiveness and extreme individuality which seems to be inherent in the national disposition and which prevents us from uniting sufficiently on any given issue to carry it through against a more unified and less disputatious and hair-splitting opposition. In the long run, the Scots, always fighters, seem to prefer to fight each other than the obvious foe. Toss a theory or proposition of the intellect, however abstract or far-fetched, into any group of Scotsmen and they will drop what they are doing and go to worry at it, like hungry dogs with a bone – whereas the English and most other groups would either smile, shrug or yawn with boredom, and resume their chat. This, in the individual, can of course lead to inventions, discoveries, innovations, the triumph of ideas – but in the mass, in the nation, can lead to chronic inertia, the cancelling-out of initiatives, stalemate and consequent defeat. In other words, we are brilliant at winning charges, quite good at battles, but not at winning wars.

There is more to it than this, admittedly. There seems to be a sort of flaw in our corporate nature which positively embraces misfortune, not exactly a death-wish but a preoccupation with disaster, a fatalism and national pessimism. Also a resentment against any of our fellows who stand out in any way as better or more successful than ourselves – the 'him – I ken't his faither!' attitude – which has had a grievous effect on our public life and sent many of our brightest and best out of the country. Why should this be? I cannot hazard a guess. It is not a sense of inferiority – although we are often accused of this; the reverse, almost, for there is no question that the average Scot at heart considers that he, individually, is a pretty fine production – just as the Englishman does not have to consider that his *race* is the salt of the earth. Somewhere therein lies our governmental failure, I suggest.

Before we consider how ill-done-by we are through being governed from four-hundred miles away by folk not of our own race and who don't understand us or wish to, let us take just a glance at how we governed ourselves before 1707. For the seeds of our present situation may have been germinated then and history has a habit of repeating itself. Who knows, a similar situation might arise if ever we do get round to taking our fate into our own hands again, in whatever degree.

The Scottish governmental system, which evolved more or less naturally down the centuries, had its strengths and its weaknesses, inevitably. But it was probably apt for the people it governed, minimal in its impact, not much trouble to anyone, the reverse of strong in fact. I do not say that it was democratic, but then, what government was in those days? At least it was not dictatorial, bureaucratic nor indeed very efficient, and allowed folk to go mostly their own way – which suited the Scots. It started, recognisably as government, with the old Pictish-Celtic dynastic rule, a modified kingship, not an all-powerful one. The title of King of the Picts, later King of Scots, is significant – not like King of England, King of France or King of Spain. King of Scots implies that he was the *leader* of the Scots not the master or owner of the land – the clan-chief idea writ large, patriarchal not feudal. Also he was High King, which implies lesser kings; and that was the system. The High King was elected, from the royal house, by the lesser kings or *ri*, choosing the most suitable and useful candidate available, not necessarily the eldest heir. These *ri* were the mormaors or hereditary rulers of the seven great divisions of Alba or Pictavia – Moray,

Ross, Mar, Atholl, Angus, Strathearn and Fife – which mormaors later became the Seven Earls of Scotland, and to which was added in due course Buchan and The Lennox. These constituted the Council of the Seven Earls, which not only elected the *Ard Righ* or High King but had an important influence over him. He had to carry the majority of the earls, in peace as in war, or he was in trouble. So, from the first, there was a governor on the engine of supreme power.

Out of this developed the constitutional system of the King in Council, later the King in Parliament, and this subsisted right up until the Union. This was the ruling body, the King *in* Parliament – not as in England and now the United Kingdom, of the King *outside* Parliament. In Scotland the monarch was part of parliament, and sat in at its sessions. He did not conduct it; that was the duty of the Chancellor or chief minister. He had to be there, or it was no Parliament, only a Convention. This was important, for it meant not only that the doings of the ruler could be debated and controlled, but also that the King's presence and influence could keep power-hungry individuals and groups from becoming too strong, on the governmental scene at least. The parliamentary make-up itself was admittedly less than democratic, and known as the Three Estates, of lords, country or shire representatives and churchmen – the last superseded after the Reformation by burgh representatives. The lords in the first instance could only be appointed by the crown; the county representatives were elected by fairly small numbers of their fellow-lairds and land-holders; the clerics were a law unto themselves but often spoke quite effectively for the common folk; and the burgh members were usually provosts, magistrates and deacons of craft and merchant guilds, not directly elected. So the Scots Parliament could not be said to be a democratically representative body by present standards; but it did broadly act in the interests of the more substantial sections of the population and tended to leave the rest alone. Parliaments tended to be few, not even always once a year.

This system had its benefits of non-interference and of keeping

Portrait of James the Sixth and First – probably flattering

the rulers under fair control. But it had its weaknesses too – and the worst was revealed when, in 1603, James the Sixth succeeded to the throne of Elizabeth Tudor and went off promptly to London. So the king-pin of the King in Parliament was removed, and though represented thereafter by appointed High Commissioners sent up, it was never the same. It allowed the rule of favourites, and all sorts of misgovernment and nepotism. Everything which required the royal favour and assent had to be petitioned for in London – and the Scots nobility began to beat a trail to the South and the source of preferment. Moreover the monarchs, from Charles the First onwards, soon discovered the advantages of the English system of creating large numbers of new lords, which in England only gave them control of the House of Lords but in the Scottish set-up could give control of the entire Parliament, since all sat together in one assembly. It was a bad day for Scotland when Elizabeth died and left James Stewart as her nearest heir. When, a century later, the Treaty of Union was foisted upon Scotland, there were one-hundred-and-fifty-three lords voting as against only eighty-five shire representatives and sixty-seven of the burghs – many of the lords newly-created. Needless to say most voted as their master – or in this case their mistress, Queen Anne, commanded. With the aid of vast bribery, the Union was voted through – an end of an auld sang indeed.

Since then we have had long-range government, frequently benevolent in intention – although by no means always so – but seldom really *interested*, seldom well-informed, seldom very effective. It is hardly to be wondered at. The Scots elected membership of the House of Commons is seventy as against six-hundred-and-fifty; and the impact of these seventy is largely nullified by the prevailing two-party system where one half cancels the other out. Also, since to be a Scots M.P. in an assembly four hundred and more miles away is very much a full-time job, only those who really desire to make a career of politics stand for election – which of course debars many of the most able and effective and successful from standing, since it would mean giving up their normal lives and businesses. So we have, by and large, achieved only a pretty mediocre standard of representatives, to our loss; and these, if they wish for promotion and office, as politicians will, must inevitably

ever, bills brought before Westminster seeking self-government again, in some degree or other. These, to be sure, could be guaranteed to fail in the vote, by the enormous English majority, or never even get that far, unless some state of national or political stress and balance required that the Scots be temporarily placated. The Liberal Party has been consistent in its support for self-government, on federal lines, even if not very effective about it – which was why I eventually joined the Liberals, although I was brought up a 'good Conservative'. In 1913 one such bill, with a Liberal government, did gain the necessary assent – but then the Great War came and the chance was lost, Scotland refusing to take the Irish road. Between the wars there were renewed efforts, none remotely successful, none with the drive of the Scots people really behind it – for with the rise of the idea of socialism, the radical Scots tended to see their duty in supporting for the time-being a United Kingdom endeavour to advance social utopia by legislation.

But after the Second World War things were rather different. A disillusionment was abroad. As I have indicated, I was not the only one who came home from the Services with eyes opened in a number of ways, especially as to Scotland's relative position. It was a time of reaction, discontents and grievous shortages, with mismanagement. The fruits of victory were hard to discern. Men who had been fighting for years were not in a mood to put up with it all meekly. All over the country pressure-groups and associations sprang up in aid of this cause or that, political, social and cultural.

Amidst all this ferment, what might be called a national movement began to develop on a number of fronts. The National Party of Scotland had been formed in 1928; but very much on the fringes of the political scene it had never gained any great strength, the mass of the people looking more towards the Labour Party, then in favour of self-government, for reform of their state. This National Party was further weakened by internal dissention, the differences in outlook and method between the firebrands and intellectuals and the more practical and 'moderate' gradualists. A split had occurred, in typical Scots fashion, and the Scottish National Party had hived off. The second war put all this largely in abeyance. But that over, it started up afresh. Opinions within the N.P.S. and the S.N.P. were as divided as ever as to methods and goals. But both gained new adherents. The Labour nationalists were also vocal. And a new influence developed, the Communists. It has to be remembered that Communism had gained a degree of recognition, almost respectability, especially amongst the young, at this time thanks to the great part played latterly by Russia in gaining victory over the Germans. The new Communist groups in Scotland were strong supporters of home rule. Unhappily, all these groupings and parties considered the others mistaken and worse.

In an effort to create some sort of common front, John M. MacCormick, a far-seeing Glasgow lawyer with a gift for oratory, one of the S.N.P. leaders, in 1942 had formed a body called Scottish Convention, with the aid of the Duke of Montrose and Sir Alexander McEwan. It was intended, not to supersede the parties, but to bridge the gaps between the inimical groups and serve as a rallying ground for the uncommitted mass of Scots in favour of self-government. The end of the war and the returning ex-Servicemen greatly boosted these movements in general. In 1945 the S.N.P. actually gained a seat in Parliament, when Dr. Robert McIntyre won the Motherwell by-election. Scottish Convention boomed also, many seeing it as the best way to unite the nation – including the present writer, brand new to the struggle, who joined it in 1947.

Convention set up branches all over the land and made quite an impact. Somehow I found myself to be Chairman of the Edinburgh branch. But I fear that it had no great effect on the political parties. However it did good educative work; and in especial established the Scottish National Assemblies, annual gatherings held in the Church of Scotland Assembly Halls, in Edinburgh. These Assemblies, although organised by the Convention, were attended by members of all parties and none, trade unions, local authorities and so on, and provided a platform and sounding-board for all concerned over the grievous state of Scotland. As such they provided the nearest thing to a representative and corporate voice of the nation to be heard since the Union – that is, except for the Church of Scotland's own General Assemblies, whose Church and Nation Committee had never ceased to uphold the idea of eventual self-government. The Kirk indeed deserves great praise for having kept the flag flying, in however minor a way, for so long. Now a notable number of ministers took part in these National Assemblies.

Out of the Assemblies, in 1949, came the Scottish Covenant – and this development took the nation so much by storm that for some months it was the main political talking-point. Scottish Convention changed its name to the Scottish Covenant Association, and devoted all its efforts to furthering this surge towards self-government. The Covenant itself was a statement comparatively brief, of the same tradition as the old National and Solemn League Covenants of the 17th century, commencing: "We, the people of Scotland who subscribe this engagement, declare . . ." and going on to affirm the need for reform in government and the securing of a parliament for Scottish affairs, within the framework of the United Kingdom, the signatories pledging themselves to do all in their power to bring this about. It was most carefully worded – I know, for I helped to word it, having been appointed Vice-Convenor of the Covenant Association – in order to command the very greatest adherence from all shades of opinion in Scotland. This, of course, held its own weaknesses, since it did not go nearly far enough for many, especially those who wished for full independence. But it did gain an extraordinarily high level of acceptance, and for most of the next year the Covenant was on everyone's lips, seldom out of the headlines and with queues lining up to sign it up and down the land, even many of the prominent and influential eager to adhere – which was something new. Over two million signatures were announced presently – which represented well over half the total Scottish electorate. It was thought that in the face of this overwhelming demand for self-government the politicians in London must surely bow to the expression of public opinion. And if they mistrusted some percentage of the Covenant signatures as bogus or repeated – as they did not fail to do – then we urged that a national plebiscite should be held to clinch the matter. We had no doubts as to the results.

We were naive, of course – but it was a near thing. A prominent politician later told some of us that had the Covenant contained a 'sanctions clause' committing the signatories to actually *voting* only for those candidates for Parliament who would demand self-government, then we would have got it, for Westminster was shaken. But no such specific voting commitment was incorporated, only the 'do all in our power' wording – and I take my full share of blame for having failed to foresee that the professional politicians would spot this loophole. We simply believed that such evidence of overwhelming support would be sufficient for honourable and fair-minded members of government to recognise that reform was democratically demanded and to do something about granting it. Well, it was not. When London perceived that the Covenant expressed only the *desire* of the Scots people, not a commitment to translate it into the only kinds of action which the powers-that-be understood, at the ballot-box or by force of some sort, they felt safe enough to do nothing, in masterly inaction. In vain thereafter the pleas, the lobbying the resolutions, the threats. Even the Stone of Destiny incident, although it set Scotland by the ears and greatly upset the highest circles, failed to bring about any positive reaction to the demand, however much of the other kind of reaction it produced, as I shall indicate hereafter. Hopes declined and the tempo of enthusiasm could not be maintained. The inevitable internal bickering commenced. The Covenant had shot its bolt and we were no further forward. The death of John MacCormick saw the demise of this effort, which had looked at one time almost sure of success.

For a while everything on the self-government front languished. The Motherwell seat was lost in Parliament and the S.N.P.'s fortunes dwindled. Then in the 1960s the national spirit picked up again, and now the S.N.P. was the beneficiary. The device of using the nationalists for protest-voting against one or other of the great

S.N.P. political meeting. Author not a party-member
but supports some of its aspirations

parties had something to do with it; but this was not the whole picture, or the Liberals would have benefited equally. Continuing frustrations with the ever-increasing centralisation of London government were mainly responsible; and the basic Scottish desire to manage their own affairs was always there – and no doubt always will be. At any rate the S.N.P. began to win seats at by-elections, to enter into local government and to build up an impressive organisation throughout the country. Outright independence was their aim, not 'devolution' or federalism.

We all know what happened. Becoming worried, Prime Minister Edward Heath suggested that some sort of modest self-government might be advisable to prevent this independence idea from gaining ground. A committee of enquiry was set up, under Lord Home the former Prime Minister, which eventually came out in modified favour. A change of government, however, resulted in a Royal Commission on the subject – for both parties were seriously alarmed over the S.N.P. successes. These two time-honoured devices were intended to delay, of course; neither Labour nor Conservative *wanted* the Scots to control their own destinies.

At last, with the political balance at Westminster more delicate than for many a day, so that even the few Liberals were keeping the Labour administration in office by means of the Lib-Lab Pact, the Scottish vote became for the moment vitally important. Labour, under Callaghan, passed the Scotland Act, whereby a referendum would be held on whether or not to set up a Scottish Assembly in Edinburgh, with very limited powers admittedly – but a step at least towards self-government. Although it was scarcely hailed by anyone with enthusiasm, not going far enough for most, not even giving any financial powers, and certainly falling a long way short of the independence campaigned for by the S.N.P., nevertheless the government assumed that it would be accepted, sufficiently for them to purchase the handsome premises of the Royal High School in Edinburgh, overlooking St. Andrew's House, the centre of administrative government, and to start converting the building to be the Assembly-hall and offices. But, as events proved, this was governmental resignation, certainly not enthusiasm.

The Referendum of March 1979 was one of the most shameful frauds ever perpetrated upon any people by an allegedly representative and democratic legislature. After the Scotland Act was passed by Commons and Lords, a more than half-empty House passed a further 'postscript' to it, initiated by a Labour member for a London constituency, one George Cunningham – a Scot, sadly – which declared that the referendum decisions must be voted for by at least forty percent of the total Scottish electorate, or the proposed reforms were to be abandoned. This was, of course, something totally new in British politics, where hitherto a simple majority vote had decided all, including seats in parliament and every government measure. That the Labour administration was prepared to accept this was ominous.

The devolution debate caused scarcely a ripple in England; but in Scotland there was much heart-burning. Although the Scotland Act was a government measure, the government itself did nothing to commend it to the Scots – it was take it or leave it, with this forty-percent time-bomb in the background. The Scottish Labour movement was half-hearted, the Conservatives were officially anti, the Liberals less than enthusiastic, the S.N.P. divided. Admittedly it was not a good Act and the proposed Assembly inadequate. But it was something, after centuries of little or nothing; and once established, any change could only be forward. To counter the strong, orchestrated and notably well-financed forces urging a No vote, a Yes for Scotland national committee was set up, on which I served, with branches throughout the land but no financial backing other than individual subscriptions. Big business was notably on the other side, as were almost all other aspects of the Establishment; but considerable enthusiasm was generated at ground level. But the forces arrayed against us were daily revealed as ever more potent. Here is no place to recount the details of that sorry episode – save perhaps to emphasise the important impact of Lord Home's broadcast urging a No vote, on the grounds that something better than this Assembly was required and would in due course be produced by a Conservative administration. Lord Home's reputation, as a former Prime Minister, was high, especially with the Scots middle class voter. At any rate, amidst confusion, doubts, misrepresentations, ill-feeling and yes, apathy, the vote was taken. The forty-percent hurdle was not cleared, although a simple majority voted Yes. Scores of thousands fewer voted No – but a third of the entire electorate did not vote at all.

Looked at from any angle, the result was a shame and a disgrace to Scotland – as was the entire proceedings. Compared with this,

*Scene of the Scottish Assembly fraud –
the former Royal High School, Edinburgh*

the Covenant failure was an honourable and forgivable one.

The question began to be asked, not whether the Scots really wanted self-government but whether they *deserved* it?

Thereafter, the S.N.P. by using their dozen votes at Westminster, were able to bring down the Labour government on a Conservative motion of no confidence – even though that government was in theory still committed to setting up the Assembly. Whether this was a wise move is still debated. I personally wrote to the S.N.P.

members – although I had never joined that party – urging that they did not do this; not that I supported the Socialist cause, but I contended that they were still weak, and Scotland's only chances lay in putting pressure on weak Westminster administrations; whereas the government replacing them would probably be much stronger. A Conservative government was in fact then elected by a large majority – and despite Lord Home's broadcast assertions, all reference to Scottish self-government was not only omitted from the Tory programme but its spokesmen left no doubts that they considered the issue a dead duck. The S.N.P., for its part, suffered drastic defeat at the polls and ended up with only two members left.

Scotland was back at square-one again, and moreover more disillusioned and depressed than at any time I could recollect.

burden of it is rather frightening. How to go on, to keep it up, book after book, year after year? Do not mistake me – I consider it the best life that I, or anyone, could envisage and I would not change it for any other. One is one's own master, can live where one likes, within reason, can adopt an independent stance on most matters, can be as odd-ball and unconventional as one's nearest and dearest permits, own a little platform from which to express oneself – which the psychiatrists will declare is the most enviable situation known to man – and have that infinite satisfaction of creating something new every day of one's life, even if not everyone thinks it worth creating. Even though the financial rewards also are apt to be inadequate and laughably different from common assumption. But all this has to be paid for, in aloneness – I will not call it loneliness, for I think that few novelists are ever really lonely. Moreover this utter dependence on self, day in day out, can have dangerous effects on a man's character and attitudes. The author is probably apt to be a supreme egoist anyway, and this life style can reinforce that and has to be countered, the self-bit played down, the creator of all these wordy effusions constantly reminded that he is but clay like everybody else and pretty muddy clay at that often enough. So, what matters most in the present context is that he is in danger of getting out-of-touch both with reality and with his fellows. The ivory-tower mentality must be guarded against all the time, however plastic the ivory. If not, very quickly much that he writes will become practically unreadable and certainly unacceptable to most readers. I have known not a few writers who, when successful, have gone off to live in some remote or exclusive paradise, which they had always thought would be ideal – and have fairly speedily either come back again or given up writing. The corners, in other words, have to be rubbed off by association with others and the abrasions of everyday living, outwith the writer's special existence. So, to keep his feet on the ground, the author *requires* to get involved with other folk – that is, if he is a professional, living only by his pen. I perceived this fairly early on – although I suspect that I am anyway a sort of interfering

The author pontificating on a cause

and know-better character with a tendency to put my oar in unsolicited.

I got involved, then. I have mentioned the Clan Albainn Society, the road committees, the Forth Road Bridge business, Scottish Convention and the Covenant, the Aberlady Bay contest and so on. At one time, to my horror May and I counted up that I was then eleven chairmen or presidents – which goes to show that involvement can get out-of-hand. Actually, I am still distinctly over-exposed, as the phrase goes, despite determined efforts to disengage.

Although time-consuming and often unprofitable, many of these extramural activities have produced their own side-issue bonuses, even when on the face of it unsuccessful. For instance my entanglement in the Berwick for Scotland cause, although fruitless save in various small excitements, did result in my writing a novel, *Kettle of Fish*, which dealt with the allied subject of drift-netting for salmon at the mouth of the Tweed. This, in turn, brought me within hailing distance of legal proceedings.

It went like this. Anyone who knows Berwick-on-Tweed will be aware of the importance of the salmon-netting industry at the mouth of that great river. This is strictly in the hands of the Tweed Commissioners and their lessee the Berwick Salmon Fisheries Company – the Commissioners being in the main the proprietors of the river fishings, the Tweedside lairds. These were powerful enough to obtain in 1857 a special Act of Parliament, the Tweed Fisheries Act, which made it illegal to catch salmon in the river and its mouth save without the permission of these Commissioners. Well, this was a nice piece of landlordism, typical of the times, for the salmon catches were quite something, involving hundreds of thousands of pounds. However, the Act went on to define the mouth of the Tweed as extending up and down the coast from Berwick for ten miles and out to sea for another five – fifty square miles of the ocean. And this significant area was, of course, the fishing-grounds of the good fishermen of the coastal havens, Burnmouth and Eyemouth and St. Abbs to the north and Seahouses to the south. Therein they must not catch salmon, open sea as it was. The Tweed Act in fact ignored the three-mile limit for inshore fishing, so that, for this one patch of sea, the prohibited zone for *British* fishermen went out five miles, whereas foreign fishermen, under the International Convention of the Sea, could fish up to three miles from the shore – two miles by ten of water denied to the locals. Also to be considered, Scots common law says that the crown rights over salmon-fishing extend to only one mile out from the foreshore. So this Westminster Act, like so many, was contrary to Scots common law. Well, anyone can guess what the results of this would be with our sturdy Scots fisherfolk – they ignored the Act, or at least broke it when they could do so without being caught. For, after the Second War, the Tweed Commissioners invested in a fast patrol-boat – which, in fact, had belonged to Adolf Hitler, of all people – and this lesser war was on.

Perceiving the drama in all this, as well as the unfairness and folly, I began investigations and went to work on a novel of adventure and high jinks on the high seas, but with the intention of also bringing the matter into more public notice. Unfortunately or otherwise, the public were notified rather sooner and differently from my intention. For one Eyemouth skipper unwisely jumped the gun rather, and was caught drift-netting for salmon three weeks before the official opening of the salmon season – which gave the Tweed authorities scope to charge him with more than just the doubtful and controversial Tweed Act offence, but with illegal fishing out of season. This had its effect on my own position, for the book was due to come out a few weeks later and was to be serialised in a national newspaper – and of course the case had not yet come before the courts and any comment could be construed as *sub judice*, and I certainly took sides in the matter of the Tweed Act in the novel, though not on the matter of unseasonable fishing. The newspaper editor took fright and called off the serialisation – to my bank account's loss, needless to say. Fortunately my London publishers were made of sterner stuff and took a less alarmist view, especially when I went to an eminent legal luminary in Edinburgh who assured me that any competent expert on Scots law could, as he said, drive a coach and horses through the wretched Tweed Act – that is, in a *Scottish* court. In the end, nothing very dire happened to the Eyemouth skipper who was fined and his catch confiscated on the fishing-out-of-season charge, the rest being discreetly

Eyemouth and fishing-fleet. Somewhat involved in salmon drift-net war

back-pedalled. So the night-time drift-netting continued, probably the patrol-boat was told not to be too enthusiastic – and no doubt the publicity all helped the sale of the book.

Incidentally the Tweed Act still stands, the surreptitious drift-netting goes on still and every now and again there is some outcry in the Berwick area. I suppose I may have managed to ventilate the matter in some small measure but certainly not enough to have the Act done away with – and I almost certainly trod on some lairdly toes along the Tweed in the process.

One other little point, harking back to the Berwick for Scotland cause, which started it all. Berwick was originally Scotland's greatest seaport and, naturally, the county town of Berwickshire. The fact that England took it and held it by force of arms is only a doubtful right in law today. But what I want to emphasise is that, for the purposes of the said Tweed Act of 1857, amended 1859, the entire River Tweed including the south as well as the north banks, was deemed to be a *Scottish* river and any infringements of the Act to be judged by Scots law. Which makes rather a nonsense of Berwick, on the north bank as it is, being part of the county of Northumberland, doesn't it?

Then the Aberlady Bay case, showing up some more follies and inconsistencies in the law as passed by Westminster in casual fashion, with dangers to public rights – always a concern of mine – I decided to deal with this situation via the novel also. However, having occasional moments of discretion – and a wise wife – and with three political lawlords, not to mention the local sheriff involved, I elected to set my story right on the other side of Scotland, in far Kintyre, just in case anyone thought that they might see some sort of significant parallels. I called this one *Ducks and Drakes* and sought to give it a light-hearted touch. It was my twenty-first novel published.

Needless to say, the press, in reports and reviews, ignored my discretion and gleefully dragged in the suggestion that it all referred of course to the Aberlady Bay rumpus, this almost unanimously. The story was first serialised in the *Bulletin*, a newspaper now sadly defunct; and even it advertised the thing as not unconnected with Aberlady. So much for authorly circumspection. But no dire repercussions followed. When the book itself came out I sought to stiffen some of the more obviously thin ice by holding a launching party in the North British Hotel, Edinburgh, to which, as well as the press, I invited some of the wildfowler protagonists, my legal adviser and counsel and two senior members of the opposition, from the Scottish Ornithologists Club who had been active on the mud-flats – these as well as some less combative guests, even if no lawlords. It made an inspiriting evening. I don't think that either

Glen Feshie, with private road only, and footbridge

side converted the other, but at least we did not actually come to blows – and having partaken of my salt, the good bird-watchers could hardly thereafter take drastic proceedings against me. I don't think, mind you, that they appreciated it when Moray McLaren – since sorrowfully deceased – called them ornithosophists.

Another of my ploys which did not come off was the Glen Feshie Road campaign. This, oddly enough, got more national publicity than other and less ambitious but more successful ventures, even the then highly popular London magazine, *Picture Post* taking the thing up. The idea, which was by no means new – indeed General Wade in the 18th century had planned this road – was to link

Glen Feshie – no road this way

Aberdeenshire and the North-East with the West Highland coast by means of a new 26-mile highway from Linn o' Dee, where the Deeside road ends, through the south-eastern Cairngorm foothills by Glen Geldie to Glen Feshie, and so down that beautiful valley to the A9 at Kingussie and Newtonmore, whereafter the A86 carries on through the Monadh Liath mountains by Laggan and Spean Bridge to Fort William and salt-water. There is already a road down much of Glen Feshie, but this is private to the shooting-lodge and kept locked. Actual new roadway from Linn o' Dee to Glenfeshie Lodge would be around 16 miles, and admittedly it would require some major engineering – but, as I say, nothing which old Wade could not contemplate and no worse than the A9 over the Pass of Drumochter or the Lecht road to Tomintoul. In fact it is astonishing that there was – and still is – no east-west through-highway across Scotland between the Perth-Oban one and the Spey-Laggan one, a gap of over seventy miles. Surely it would be hard to find any other comparable hiatus in the road-system of these islands, even in the far north. And such a link was important, for more than travellers and tourists. For more and more east-coast fishing-fleets have to operate out of the West Highland ports of Mallaig, Ullapool and Kinlochbervie, and the fishermen have to get home at week-ends to Aberdeen, Peterhead, Fraserburgh and the rest; also the fish-lorries have to bring their cargoes to the east-coast markets.

Knowing Feshie and Geldie so well, I took up this fight because of the obvious need, and because of the magnificent and almost unknown empty country it would open up to visitors, for the head of Feshie in especial is tremendous in scale and dramatic qualities; the yawning abyss of Coire Garbhlach, surely one of the most impressive corries in the land; the remote and exciting course of the River Eidart, perhaps the least-known major stream in Scotland; and the Feshie itself, unique in its riparian thuggery in stealing the headwaters of the east-flowing River Geldie, by a backward-cutting process, and so enormously increasing its own west-flowing importance. Moreover, the Cairngorm National Park was then being proposed and this road would greatly enhance that project.

Alas, despite all the eloquence and agitation, masterly inactivity on the part of government ensured that nothing was done – and at least some folk were happy, including my old music teacher at Heriot's School, Dr. W. B. Moonie, who wrote to the *Scotsman:* "Why should the motorist be handed on a plate these glories of the Scottish Highlands which have up till now been the reward of the virile man and the big-hearted woman?" And another enthusiast, from Dundee, asserted that: "All articles on the road problem ought to state plainly that anyone who decided to buy or use a car (or anyone who fails to break an already acquired habit of unnecessary use) is increasing the accident risks of the community; and that no government expenditure whatsoever can counteract that increase."

At any rate all the publicity, however ineffective, was instrumental in bringing me and my little efforts to the notice of sundry high-powered road, tourist and haulage interests in London, who at this stage, 1956, were campaigning strongly for major reforms in the road-system, its financing, and for the setting up of a National Highway Authority. I was asked to spearhead this effort in Scotland; and at the same time to compile and have illustrated the Scottish edition of the British Road Federation's booklet entitled *Roads Matter*. I was actually paid for this, the first and only occasion that I ever made any money out of my campaigning, save for payment for journalistic articles – and the fact that it came from London was added satisfaction.

But despite the efforts of big business in the South and a small novelist in Scotland, no Highway Authority eventuated, any more than did the Glen Feshie road. But I did achieve a 1300-mile tour of inspection of Scottish roads, from the Mull of Galloway to Cape Wrath – during which, whatever else, we managed to visit and draw practically every small castle in the land. Somehow this seemed to make it all worth while.

My investigations into the Feshie, Geldie and Eidart river systems much helped in my writing of the novel of hydro-electrics, *The Chosen Course*.

The Covenant self-government campaign involved me in various side-issues, the most colourful of which undoubtedly was the Stone of Destiny business. Not that the Covenant Association was directly implicated, although some of its leading figures were. My connection was, in the first instance, purely adventitious and at second-hand. I had, in the November of 1950, published my novel *The Freebooters*, already referred to; and in this, amongst the ploys discussed by the characters for waking up Scotland, was a suggestion that the Stone of Scone might be abstracted from its Coronation-chair in Westminster Abbey and brought back to Scotland, from which it had been purloined by Edward the First seven hundred years before. I, or they, did not take this theme any further than the mere proposal, for in fact I was not convinced that the Coronation Stone was the true Lia Fail, the semi-legendary Stone of Destiny, of Ireland, Dalriada and Scone Abbey, suspecting it to be a mere lump of Scone sandstone, quarried there either for or by Edward Plantagenet in 1296. More of that later.

However, when on Christmas night Ian R. Hamilton, a young lawyer and friend of mine on the Covenant Committee, abetted by some Glasgow student friends, most dramatically did indeed take the Stone from Westminster, in a feat which hit the headlines everywhere, it was perhaps natural for it to be suspected that I, or at least my novel, had something to do with it, *The Freebooters* having been serialised in the *Daily Mail* – although in fact, Ian assured me later that he had not read of it beforehand and the affair

The author's sketch of his idea of true Stone of Destiny, as described by early chroniclers

was entirely coincidental. As it happened, I got very prompt news, of a sort, of the event; for that same night I had a late 'phone call from our Chief Constable, with whom I was friendly, informing me cryptically that I might be wise to tidy up my rock-garden at Aberlady as it might possibly prove to be of interest to visitors! I was mystified – although it was not long before I became all too well aware of the situation.

The Stone had been taken from the Coronation-chair in Westminster Abbey, and the Dean thereof was crying that it was sacrilege and a senseless crime. The government was scandalised, with the English Home Secretary, Chuter Ede, vehement in condemnation. It was clearly a Scottish nationalist outrage. I was known to be, if not a nationalist, at least a campaigner for self-government. I had written this book in which the thing was suggested. Therefore it was obvious that I was involved. The telephone never stopped ringing, the press, the BBC, friends, neighbours, relations, colleagues in the Covenant Association, complete strangers. I was a great disappointment to all, knowing nothing about it.

My real connection with the incident came later, many weeks later. In the meantime the Stone had been smuggled back to Scotland, word of this had inevitably leaked out, a petition had been sent to the King, by Ian and his friends, assuring loyalty – for it was known that George the Sixth was much upset – and declaring that the Stone would be returned to His Majesty's officers on promise of it remaining in Scotland. Unfortunately Chuter Ede had sent two senior Scotland Yard men up here to find the relic – although of course they had no authority in Scotland; and the Scottish police co-operated with them only very doubtfully. The Stone, which had an ancient crack across it, had in fact broken in two when Ian dragged it out of the Coronation-chair on to the Abbey floor, and had to be mended. This was done in the monumental sculptor's yard in Sauchiehall Street, Glasgow, of Councillor, later Baillie Robert Gray, my fellow Vice Convenor of the Covenant Association, who was in the plot from the start. Thereafter it had to be moved about secretly almost every night for fear of discovery, so a lot of people were risking their reputations and possibly even their freedom by giving it house-room – and a substantial visitor it made, weighing some hundredweights. The fear of its capture was not so much from the police but from a small group of extreme nationalists of republican sympathies who were determined that on no account should the Stone go back to London. They had a motor-boat hired and waiting, and were allegedly intending to grab the thing, take it out to sea, and sink it in the deeps of the Firth of Clyde. These people, being considerably more knowledgeable about the nationalist scene and personnel than were the detectives, were much nearer to laying hands on the precious lump of masonry, indeed they were believed to be only two jumps behind its frequent removals.

As I have said, the Covenant Association was no wise involved in all this, even though some of its leaders had now become so. But inevitably many folk thought that it was all a Covenant publicity ploy, and almost certainly the authorities, especially in London, thought the same. In one way we benefited, of course, for the whole affair gave a boost to the Scottish national spirit; but we also were suffering somewhat in reputation as a moderate, law-abiding and responsible quasi-political movement, committed to use only constitutional methods. And if in fact the Stone was taken by those republicans, dumped in the sea and lost for ever, there would be grievous repercussions. After all, for seven hundred years every monarch of England and later of the United Kingdom, had been crowned on it.

It was in these circumstances that I was drawn in. The Covenant Committee rightly or wrongly came to the decision that any good in the Stone's purloining was now achieved and that there was a grave risk of serious harm to the cause if the relic remained in limbo. We too were concerned that it should not be whisked off to London again, if brought to light. But John MacCormick was friendly with Hector MacNeil, the Socialist Secretary of State for Scotland – who, needless to say, had been not a little put out by the way his Cabinet colleague, the Home Secretary, with no responsi-

Charles L. Warr, Dean of the Thistle and minister of St. Giles, and the then Dean of the Faculty of Advocates. This little group got together in the Moncrieffes' Edinburgh house, and all agreed that the Stone must be brought out in a safe and suitable fashion – especially as now the government was considering prosecutions. How and where? The how I thought could be arranged; but the where was a problem. St. Giles Kirk, the first and obvious location, was ruled out by Dr. Warr. The church was under surveillance it seemed, by police, day and night; for letters to the press had advocated it as being the best place for the Stone to appear – and the C.I.D. headquarters were next-door. Indeed the assistant organist, poor man, had been arrested the previous evening on suspicion as he entered the kirk. Holyroodhouse and its ruined abbey were well-guarded. It was felt that since the Stone had been removed from a consecrated building it would be apt and right for it to reappear in another. Dunfermline Abbey, which has played a resounding part in Scots history and where the Bruce's body lies, was suggested, as was St. Mungo's Cathedral, Glasgow; but Dr. Warr pointed out that both were still places of worship with ministers responsible, and it was unfair to involve any clergyman in the Stone's handing-over to the authorities, as he might well thereafter be the recipient of much abuse from the uninformed and unthinking as a betrayer of Scotland's cause. Then our legal Dean hit on the idea of Arbroath Abbey. This, of course, was the scene of the magnificent Declaration of Independence signing, in 1320; but it was now a ruin and in the care of H. M. Office of Works and would not be guarded at night-time – highly important if the deliverers of the massive freight were not to be apprehended and arrested.

We were all delighted with this solution as to where. But the question of how remained. It was late at night and in the next day's edition of the *Scotsman* there would be a letter from the Master of Belhaven, one of the Covenant Committee, urging that the Stone be brought out and delivered to the High Constable, the Countess of Erroll, as suitable custodian and first in precedence in Scotland after the royal family. Lady Erroll, still only in her early twenties,

St. Giles High Kirk, Edinburgh – cathedral a misnomer. The Stone might have rested here

was much alarmed at the thought of the Stone being dumped on her doorstep in Carlton Terrace and what the mob might do then. We all helped her to draft a letter also, saying that she did not want the relic delivered to her, but that it should be put in some suitable and sacred public place and with dignity. She likewise urged the authorities to act with dignity and restraint.

Now to let John MacCormick know – for though he did not know, nor want to know, where the Stone was at any given time, he knew who *did* know. Unfortunately his house was being watched by police and his telephone believed to be monitored. I did try to 'phone him without mentioning either Stone or Arbroath Abbey; but I am afraid that it was not so easy as I would have made it appear in a novel. I declared that it was the Society of Authors 'phoning and asked how about making a visit to certain ancient shrines, when members came to Scotland; and what about starting with the Declaration place? Not unnaturally John did not have a clue, and may well have wondered, at that hour of night, whether I had abandoned my lifelong teetotalism. I gave up the attempt and said that I was coming through to see him, instead.

So leaving the others, Wilfred and I drove the forty miles through to Glasgow, to arrive at Park Quadrant about 2 a.m., where police kept guard at John's door. Getting into the house was tricky, not only on account of the law but because John apparently already had another visitor whom he did not want us to meet. There was a certain amount of dodging between rooms. The first visitor turned out not to be anyone of import; but we had barely got started on our tale when the doorbell rang again and we were hustled back under cover. This presumably was the caller expected. We had a long wait, for it was somebody senior from the *Daily Express* not unconnected with Hector MacNeil, with news about probable government orders to prosecute. Eventually he went, and we were able to give the Lord Rector of Glasgow University our message.

Dr. MacCormick was delighted with the Arbroath idea and thought that all could be contrived as planned. A little time would be required, however, and time was short, with things moving to a climax.

Arbroath Abbey where the Stone of Destiny was restored to public gaze
all too briefly

Next day the letters duly appeared in the*Scotsman,* amidst much speculation; and I think that it was two nights later that Councillor Gray uplifted the Stone from an address in Stirlingshire, had it stowed in the boot of his car, and later picked up Ian Hamilton and one of his student collaborators and they drove through the April night to Arbroath in Angus, a long drive. It was daylight before they arrived but managed to find their way into the grounds of the ruined abbey with their heavy burden, something that I would like to have seen. A uniformed custodian duly turned up, but on being told what it was, shook hands with the newcomers. They left Scotland's ancient talisman – if it *was* that, and not a 700-year-old fake – under the saltire flag of Scotland, before the high altar where the Declaration had been signed twenty-four years after the Stone was taken from Scone.

All were much moved; for whatever the rights and wrongs of this entire episode, the principals therein were actuated throughout purely by patriotic motives, sincerely felt. And they were not sure, even now, whether they were in fact doing the right thing.

The sequel revealed their doubts to be well-founded. The police of course had to be informed. And they, with unseemly haste, removed the Stone to Forfar police-station and locked it up in a cell. And there the two Scotland Yard men came for it, commandeered a Black Maria, and set off for London with it the same night – taking their orders of course from Chuter Ede, the Home Secretary, not from Hector MacNeil.

So much for the position of Secretary of State for Scotland. When apologists for the present governmental arrangements declare that administrative devolution is adequate for Scotland's needs and so long as we have our own Secretary of State in the Cabinet we are all right, I remember the Stone. When the old horse falters, there is no doubt who cracks the whip.

There were no arrests, at least, although black marks were no doubt put against a number of names. They may well be there still.

There were not a few black marks debited against the Covenant leadership too, by the ordinary folk of Scotland, as stories circulated – folk who had not had to make the decision. Were *they* right, or were we?

chapter six
MORE INVOLVEMENT

I suppose that a psychiatrist, even the more discerning reader, could possibly trace a connecting theme in all, or most, of the ploys and activities I have been engaged in 'extra-murally' down the years – land-resettlement, self-government, Berwick-for-Scotland, roads, drift-netting, public rights, public-lending-right and so on. But I cannot honestly say that I myself could link them up in any reasonable way, certainly not set them down in any deliberate policy-line or sequence, satisfactory as it would be to seem so far-seeing, methodical and wise. To me, causes just seem to crop up, demanding my adherence – all very *ad hoc* and spontaneous. I imagine that the fact of the matter is that one thing succeeded another largely just *because* there was a gap, a hiatus, and I seemed to require something other than just writing and day-to-day family life to get my teeth into. All of which does not make me sound a very admirable sort of person, I admit. But then, heaven preserve me from admirable persons!

Probably therefore, the rise of the Forth road-bridge campaign grew quite naturally out of the decline of the Covenant. The Covenant Association was still very much in being when, late in 1953, I took the lead in setting up the National Forth Road Bridge Committee. Indeed it was under the auspicies of the South-East Area of the Covenant that the thing was launched, although it very quickly took its own separate identity. The fact was that the Covenant surge was petering out, once the great signatures effort had come to naught, the Queen's Title legal case had been rejected – whereby John MacCormick and a number of us sought to contest in the Scottish courts the obviously erroneous assumption for Scotland, and indeed for the United Kingdom also, of Elizabeth the Second as Her Majesty's style, when there had been no Elizabeth the First, save on the purely English former throne – and Dr. MacCormick's health and leadership were failing. So there was a period of marking-time, as so often in Scottish life, and marking-time, for an impatient character such as I fear I am, is irksome. It seems that I have to be forever marching somewhere or other. As I say, not altogether admirable.

The idea of a road-bridge over the Firth of Forth at Queensferry, alongside the rail-bridge, was not new of course, the need painfully obvious. It had been mooted thirty years earlier, and there had been agitations in the 1930s, but the Second World War halted these. Now, in 1953, complaints to the press, by various Fifers, at the ever-lengthening queues for the ferryboats, as motor traffic increased, with delays of up to two hours making it actually quicker often to turn round and drive the forty-mile detour via Kincardine Bridge – not to mention my own frequent frustrations there – spurred me on. With MacCormick's agreement, the South-East Area Council of the Covenant Association, which had superseded the Edinburgh Committee, called a great protest-meeting in the Central Halls, Edinburgh, after suitable press preparation.

It was a major success, the hall packed, reporters there in force, the platform-party impressive, and messages of support read out from high and low. Appropriately, Provost J. A. Lawson of South Queensferry took the Chair. Amidst much enthusiasm the National Forth Road Bridge Committee was formed to head up a strong

South Queensferry before the Forth Road Bridge

campaign. I was made Chairman, and had as Vice Chairmen Sir Andrew Murray, former Lord Provost of Edinburgh, and the aforementioned Provost Lawson of South Queensferry, with committee-members representative of a wide range of interests, political, trade-union, legal, business and of course local authority, with the provosts of not a few Fife burghs, such as Inverkeithing, Burntisland, Leslie and St. Monans. We forthwith appealed for a substantial fighting-fund. In this last we did rather well, money coming in from a wide variety of sources, firms and individuals. Twenty-three burghs supported us. It is worth noting that Edinburgh Town Council did not, nor did Glasgow. But far-away Stornoway sent us £5.

So commenced four years of very active campaigning, meetings public and private, deputations – I even went to London to speak to the British Road Federation – articles, letters to the press, advertisements, posters, lobbying M.P.s, stumping the country, fund-raising efforts, fetes, fairs and sales. It would scarcely have been possible to have had a better Committee, more willing and enthusiastic helpers, from our decorative but highly efficient secretary, Eleanora K. S. Grant, the brothers Mackenzie, Alastair and Hector, a former Under Secretary of State for Scotland, J. J. Robertson, Tom Oswald, M.P. for Central Edinburgh, John G. Wilson Q.C., our former counsel in the Aberlady Bay case and then Chairman of the Scottish Liberal Party, Sir Compton Mackenzie and many others. My two Vice Chairmen were towers of strength – which is not always the case – especially considering that they were both busy public figures. Provost Lawson's unfailing support was especially praiseworthy in that it was given in the face of considerable local opposition, for many South Queensferry people, traders in especial, feared that a bridge skied high above the town, would carry trade away – and of course they would lose the catering for the long queues of cars and lorries.

Opposition was not confined to South Queensferry and the nearby estate of Dalmeny on whose ground the approaches would have to be built and so might impair amenity. Dunfermline shopkeepers on the other side of the Forth were equally doubtful, on the grounds that with Edinburgh suddenly becoming a mere dozen miles or so away by road, Dunfermline folk might stream away there to shop and do business. It was an uphill task trying to convince these good people that the reverse would apply and that they would win trade, with vastly more visitors coming to Dunfermline – which we later were assured proved accurate. Then, of course, there was the usual Scots dissentient brigade to contend with who felt the necessity to contest something, anything, so long as it was being strongly advocated by others. And there were plenty to declare that a Forth road-bridge was quite unnecessary and a waste of public money, especially the sort who seldom travelled anywhere anyway. Also, to be sure, the West of Scotland and Glasgow in the main were supremely uninterested. Lastly and worst, as government opposition was made entirely evident, there was the massive weight of the establishment against the project and all the folk who habitually looked southwards for a lead, preferment and approval, something one has to reckon with always.

So, it was by no means a walk-over. But the Scottish press was largely with us, as so often I found with my efforts, for which I have reason to be suitably grateful; and East of Scotland public opinion was on the whole unswerving. The government eventually could not ignore it all. They wriggled, the Minister of Transport suggesting first that perhaps private enterprise and money might tackle the job – and then changing that tune with a change of Minister. Next it was suggested that a tube across the Forth might be better and less expensive – although that, of course, would take a long time to consider and prospect, geology and the like to be taken into account. We quickly laughed that time-wasting device out of court. So, at long last, London capitulated. The Forth Road Bridge would be built, at an estimated cost of £15 millions – instead of the £3½ millions when we started – and work would commence in 1958.

Great was the rejoicing – and amongst the most thankful was my dear May, who now hoped that she might see a bit more of her errant husband before he got caught up in the next spasm.

Such a huge structure and engineering challenge took a long time to construct, of course – after all it was the longest suspension bridge in Europe and the fourth largest in the world, demanding 210,000 tons of concrete and 35,000 tons of steel, with 10 miles of new roads, much dual-carriageway, fourteen lesser bridges, viaducts and octopus fly-overs the first in Scotland. It was 1964 before

The Forth Road Bridge under construction – the temporary aerial walkway

at length it was finished and in lofty grace it spanned the mile or so of water which had proved such a barrier to travel since Queen Margaret's time. It gave me great satisfaction to be one of the first to cross it, on foot, other than the builders, when my friend Willie Merrilees, the Chief Constable, invited me, with Mr. John Hamilton the Resident Engineer, later knighted, to walk across to Fife one breezy day in 1963. Such may sound a very modest excitement to the traveller today – but this was before the roadway-deck was built and we had to climb up and down the great suspension cables by a swinging catwalk, up to the tops of the huge 512-feet towers – although going down the other sides was worse – with the wrinkled sea far below and nothing to hang on to but a single slender wire handrail which gave and jumped. It was great fun, however – fortunately I have a good head for heights, as had Willie. It almost had to be postponed because of the breeze, for up there it can be dangerous in a wind, with the high supporting-towers necessarily having to be able to sway through quite a few feet to withstand the pressure. It took us quite a long time to cover that mile or so – and we returned on the ferry. May, who had waited at South Queens-ferry, was thankful to see us back.

So I had my own little bridge-opening and satisfyingly dramatic it was. Just as well, too, for when a year later came the offical opening by the Queen, I was not invited. Sixteen thousand invitations no less had gone, many to as far away as Canada and the U.S., and practically all the establishment figures were there who had for so long actually opposed the building of the bridge, sitting now with a quiet glow of satisfaction – I watched them, on TV – a splendid occasion. Five hundred of them were honoured by dining with the Queen afterwards. My two Vice Chairmen, like the Chief Constable, were there in other capacities. Afterwards they told me that they were astonished not to see me, and assumed that I must have fallen ill and could not attend. Mind you, it was a very official affair, with the due authorities now firmly in charge. I can understand their point of view.

Wilfred Taylor wrote a poem about it all, published in next day's

The author watching official opening of Forth Road Bridge – on television

Scotsman. I think he has done finer work, you know. It went:
  "Where's Nigel Tranter? Not at this birth,
    He toiled so hard to span the Firth;
  Sir Andrew Murray at his side,
    His time he spared it, not the tide . . ."
By this time, sadly, John MacCormick had died and Scotland was

the loser. Although the Covenant Association limped on without him for a while, I think that we all knew that it would not long survive its founder, in the climate of opinion then prevailing. The national cause would rise again – but for the moment it was in low water.

Most of my Covenant colleagues joined the Scottish National Party – and I think proved to be a source of strength and moderation. For myself, I could not feel that this was the answer. Outright independence for Scotland was the party's declared aim and I did not believe that this was what the country needed at that time; and even more, perhaps, it was not what the mass of the people would support. I wanted Scotland to become a self-governing part of the United Kingdom, managing its own domestic affairs but leaving foreign policy, defence and the crown to the Westminster government. This was what the Covenant had advocated, indeed stated in its wording; and it was what the Liberal Party stood for. Also, the Scottish Liberals were a great deal more help in the Forth road-bridge effort than were the S.N.P. John G. Wilson was their Chairman and Sir Andrew Murray was also prominent in the party, as was my good friend Andrew Haddon. I decided to join the Liberals – without any major conviction or enthusiasm, I must admit. The fact of the matter was that I was not, and am still not, politically-minded. If this seems odd, for one so apt to get involved in causes and campaigns, it should be recognised that these were each and all for a specific objective, not politically-motivated. Even the self-government movement, as far as I was concerned, came into that category. I suppose, if you define politics as the art and practice of government, then it was playing politics to try to change the governmental structure. But I was not in the least concerned with *party*-politics and expressed no views on what complexion of government ruled Scotland eventually, Right, Left or Centre, so long as it was the Scots who elected it. I fear that I have always, therefore, made a distinctly feeble Liberal – although I was appointed President of the Berwick and East Lothian Liberals in 1960, and remained so for over fifteen years. I resigned from this position, as it happened, partly because they had had long enough of me, but also because of my self-government attitude, the very cause which made me join them. I still put this first, by a long way. It was still the policy of the Liberal Party but, as I indicated earlier, on another subject, East Lothian has, shall we say, had the advantage of a large influx of English folk, and some of these proved to be Liberals – and keen Liberals at that, but not keen Scottish self-government enthusiasts, perhaps not unnaturally. So I began to find myself out-of-step with members of my Committee, who thought that I was more nationalist than Liberal. Perhaps they were right. Anyway, it was time that I went.

At various times I have been asked to stand as parliamentary candidate. Thank goodness I never agreed – although I have to thank my May too, who was strongly against it. If I had ever been elected, I would have been miserable at Westminster. But I know that I have been criticised for this, as for many other things.

I did get involved again in the ill-fated Referendum confidence-trick of 1979. I had strongly urged the setting up of a national plebiscite on the demand for self-government back in 1950, so I could hardly refuse to co-operate when I was asked to join the Yes for Scotland National Committee in 1978. Thereon I met some old friends and made some new ones – and was delighted amongst these to find Professor Neil MacCormick, John's son, whom I had last seen as a schoolboy in Park Quadrant, Glasgow. Now he was a leading light in the S.N.P. and his brother was M.P. for Argyll. I do not usually feel my age, but I did then. I greatly admired what I saw and heard of Neil. John would be proud of him. I shall say no more about the results of *that* campaign, out of which Scotland came with only a little less discredit than did the politicians.

There is another aspect of involvement in public affairs in which I have always been concerned and in which I feel that a great many of my fellow-citizens ought to be involved, on however modest a scale and however minor the aims and objects seem to be compared with building a multi-million-pound bridge, making a new road or obtaining reform in our government and the like – this is in fighting the constant threat to public rights.

This is something in which almost everyone can and should engage, to some degree. And the need is great. Today, for various reasons, the public's age-old and basic rights, often in common law, are under pressure as never before – the obstruction of rights of way, prohibitions of access to lands, multiplication of bye-laws, banning of angling and other sporting rights, closing of foreshores, proliferation of prohibiting notice-boards and many more. The increasing threat to our liberties is ominous, since the more such closures and bans are tamely accepted, the more serious grow the encroachments, nibbling away at our essential freedoms. The ever-growing centralisation of government, national and local, the vast extension of bureaucracy, the machine-age, computerisation, the expansion of multi-national conglomerates controlled from far away, the huge nationalised industries, mass media, all have the effect of limiting our local rights, even sometimes with benevolent intentions. And the people are themselves to blame often, through sheer apathy. Also, folk walk a great deal less than formerly and more and more of the population live urban lives where many of these prohibitions are scarcely noticed. Nevertheless, outdoor recreation is being pursued with ever greater enthusiasm as leisure increases and the benefits to health are publicised – hill-walking, skiing, bird-watching, boating, cycling, even jogging. All of these activities can be affected by restrictions on public rights. One would think that the Scots, of all people, would not have to be urged to stand up for their rights. But they do, probably because the menace is usually so scattered and non-publicised.

It is sad that the prime sinners in this erosion of our individual liberties so often are not wicked landowners and exclusive financial interests but our own elected representatives on district and regional councils, with their faceless employees, paid by our rates. Likewise, of course, the minions of national government, notably in the Ministry of Defence. But less lofty agencies have to be watched also – even golf clubs and the like.

While the Aberlady Bay case was the most spectacular effort in which I have engaged, there have been a number of others. Indeed the East Lothian Wildfowlers Association which we set up to help in that cause, was able to use its corporate voice in other issues where rights were threatened, including a test-case in 1961 where one of our members was charged in court by the Dalmeny estate with shooting on their land, in this case the foreshore at Dalmeny, which they claimed was private property – if I remember rightly, as far out into the tidal water as a horseman could ride, under some alleged ancient charter – but which we asserted was public domain, like all the rest of the Scottish foreshore between high and low water-mark. We won in this instance, and the legal situation was established. We also dealt with restrictive measures at Tyninghame in our own county, where admittedly there was considerable over-shooting on the foreshore and so-called 'cowboys' with guns could be a menace. This situation presented us with a salutary reminder of the fact that even in the matter of rights and liberties, the public good might not always be served by uncompromising assertion of common law. In this case we were fortunate in that the Earl of Haddington, the landowner concerned, was reasonable and in fact helpful and we were able to come to a fair and workable agreement without recourse to legalities, with concessions on both sides, the Association's members prepared to use their influence to help control the cowboys and excessive and dangerous shooting. Others than wildfowlers have rights on the foreshore, we should be the first to admit.

I have been concerned in sundry fights to retain rights-of-way, which are much at risk these days, with so many people using cars instead of their legs and old paths getting overgrown, footbridges falling down, signposts becoming defaced and so on. The Scottish Rights of Way Society does yeoman service but it has a very tiny membership. Farmers are the commonest offenders here, needless to say, often barring the way with barbed-wire, ploughing up old footpaths and even erecting notices saying "Beware of the Bull" – which can be just as effective against the timorous however imaginary the bull. Another favourite canard is a variation of the "Guard-dogs on Patrol" slogan, which indicates that fierce Alsatian dogs are at loose, so warning off the walker – regardless of the fact that if the alleged Alsatians were to attack walkers who were doing no damage to property, it would be the owners thereof who would be liable to appear in court, not the walkers. Likewise, although the position is different in England, I understand, the old "Trespassers will be Prosecuted" signs are equally a bluff, the law in Scotland requiring damage to be proved to the owner's interests for any case to be successful. The offer of a coin to a gamekeeper or other minion, to help pay for any unspecified damage, almost always spurned by the opposition, is quite a good idea, a lawyer-friend of mine told me – for you then have offered to compensate the owner for any harm he thinks you may have done by walking on his land, and it has been refused.

As I have indicated, bye-laws have to be watched carefully. The term bye-law *sounds* sufficiently authoritative; but such could be no more than irritating petty restrictions concocted by some bureaucratic department of a local council, with no basis in true law. Local authorities should be the watchdogs of the public's rights, and of course often they are. I would not like it to be thought, from all the foregoing, that I am some sort of foe of legitimate authority, local or national. Far from it. I have made common cause with local government any number of times over the years, up and down the land – particularly in the Borders, admittedly – and I recognise the important part, it has to play in the nation's life. But on occasion it can be strangely insensitive, blinkered and narrow-minded, largely in the administrative departments rather than in the councils themselves probably and vigilance is advisable.

I have been told that I have been called an agitator and busybody. Dear me, reading through all this, I wonder if that is accurate?

chapter seven
CULTURAL DABBLINGS

I hate the word culture as applied to matters of the intellect, taste and aesthetics; but strangely, alternatives are in short supply. Here, where it might be least expected, the excellent English language fails us; and in this instance our guid Scots tongue does not help to fill the gap. Which is a pity, for we need a better word; and Scotland has very much its own cultural contribution and tradition, and it would be suitable to have our own individual word for it.

As I writer I find that I am expected to be knowledgeable about things cultural, and I am afraid that I am not. Why it should be so, I am not quite sure – for I don't think that most writers are especially so, even if they manage to sound it on occasion. After all, why should a wordmonger be more knowledgeable than anybody else about paint-appliers or music-makers or ballet-dancers? None of these, I warrant, would expect to be considered expert on the novel, the poem or the play. We till our own patch and though we may have sympathies with the problems and challenges of the tillers of other patches, we seldom get hot under the collar about them, leaving this to the non-practitioners and devotees, who can make almost an industry of it – especially in Edinburgh at Festival-time.

All of which is not to say that I am not *interested* in the Scottish cultural scene in its generality. Scotland indeed has almost always had an extraordinarily rich and varied artistic expression for such a small nation, from the times of the Celtic stone-carvers, designers and sennachies onwards, in poetry, story-telling, drama, painting, architecture – a roll-call of Scots names, from Thomas the Rhymer, Barbour, Gavin Douglas, Sir David Lindsay, Allan Ramsay, Hume, Burns, Hogg, Byron, Raeburn, Adam, Carlyle, Stevenson, Scott, Barrie, Bridie, Buchan, Gunn and a hundred more, will substantiate the claim. In music we have not shone, perhaps, so brightly. The Reformation may have damped down artistic expression for a while but it picked up again and Scotland's so-called Golden Age, or the Enlightenment, was in fact a remarkable cultural flowering at a time of political declension and national insecurity after the Union. More modern times have seen a continuing development, not always sustained but sufficient to display that whilst the Scots have lagged behind in government, administration, land-use and the rest, they have retained their abilities to express themselves in artistry of varying kinds to a high degree; and given conditions in which these can be exploited, have still much to offer the rest of the world. It is a case of the individual contribution again, of course, in this race of individualists.

There is more than interest, naturally, where one's own form of expression is concerned; there is duty and a sort of accountability which ought, I feel, to involve one in some degree at least in activity on wider than the mere personal front. Not that mere is probably the right word, for the professional writer's responsibilities towards others can and should be fairly constantly on his mind. This is something which has always concerned me, sometimes almost oppressed me, as I know it does others. The writer has more opportunities than most to affect others, in thoughts and ideas and outlook, and this he has to take seriously if he has any integrity at all. The fact that he gets published means that his books are fairly

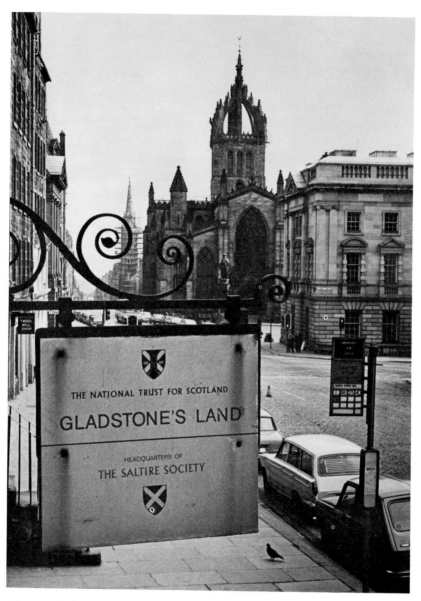

Gladstone's Land, Lawnmarket, Edinburgh,
long the headquarters of the Saltire Society

sure of a reasonably large sale, for publishers do not continue to issue books unless they are going to be read by many. The readers, with the lending libraries greatly increasing their numbers, are going to be in some measure moved, stimulated, provoked, perturbed, enfuriated or otherwise affected by what one has written, for good or ill, almost inevitably. And this can be a thought, indeed. Of course the author does not obviously preach a sermon, thump a tub, indulge in propaganda – or he would be unreadable and therefore cease to be published. Nevertheless, by inference and hints, emphasis and omission, he can subtly or otherwise influence the ideas of many. He may do it almost subconsciously; but I feel that he *ought* to know what he is doing and be prepared to live with some feeling of accountability. A writer, by the very nature of his craft, must be an enthusiast of sorts, or he would never begin to tackle the daunting task of seeking to express himself in scores of thousands of selected words. It is almost certain, therefore, that he will seek to transmit some of his enthusiasms or attitudes to other folk, even in a novel. This has to be watched. People can be affected well beyond the author's considered intent. For instance, when an early novel of mine, already mentioned, *The Chosen Course,* was fairly recently re-published, one reviewer declared that this "revealed Tranter flirting with some very dangerous ideas" – namely the blowing up of a hydro-electric project in the Highlands. This, you see, reflects *today's* attitudes to violence, after years of Terrorism, I.R.A. methods and so on; when it was written it had no such overtones – the explosion referred to actually was to alter the course of an underground river and so save a glen from being flooded. But it is an example of what I mean.

Particularly is the writer's responsibility to be emphasised in the historical novel, in which I have an especial interest. By historical, I mean not costume drama nor yet period-piece romance, where the story is the thing and being set in the past adds colour, but a genuine seeking to recount and make alive to the general reader the actualities of history and the delineation of characters who have lived and played their part in our nation's story. This involves an infinity of research, needless to say, much hard work and a major interest in character-study and motivation.

Now integrity and responsibility comes in potently here. For the author's interpretation of the characters or even the events *may* not be either the accepted or the correct one. Although, for that matter, who is to say what is the correct one? Academic historians are no more likely to be correct, even when they agree with each other, than the novelist – who at least has made a study of character-delineation and what makes people tick; add to be sure 99% of what even the most fully-documented and described characters in our history, such as Mary Queen of Scots or Bonnie Prince Charlie, said or did had not been recorded; so that there is ample scope for interpretation and informed imaginative reconstruction. Nevertheless, the said academics seldom approve of the historical novel, declaring them to give a false impression, to twist facts and so mislead. One professor went so far as to declare that what I wrote was in fact a lot of damned lies. I asked him how did he *know* that it was lies? Could he prove that I was wrong? He could not, of course. He could only quote history-books written by other academics which in turn quote each other and all eventually go back to the same accepted source-material, usually early chroniclers and their interpreters. I have to read all these too, naturally. But the point I make is – who wrote the received source-material in the first place, and why? Usually the winners wrote it, the losers being safely dead. It is almost as simple as that, often. So we are apt to get very one-sided history, the winners' side. In other words, much received history is ancient propaganda. And a lot of it is nonsense, as anyone with a close knowledge of geography and topography and some idea of tactics, for instance, can prove – for so much of it was written down at third and fourth hand by monkish chroniclers who never stirred outside their own monasteries and had not been near the terrain concerned, the monks being practically the only people who could write in those days. Innumerable victories and defeats have been won and lost, on parchment, in quite impossible terms and conditions but are sol-

Bannockburn – the actual burn, where the battle was deliberately fought down in the undrained swamps, to bog-down the English heavy cavalry

emnly accepted as truth and taught to generation after generation of students. Even Bannockburn itself is so misrepresented and makes nonsense out of Bruce's tactics. The alleged battlefield site and all its embellishments and publicity-material is not where the battle was fought at all, only where, on the high ground, Bruce *assembled* his forces. The epic struggle took place two miles away, deliberately, in the low, marshy ground of the pows or pools of Forth, where the Pelstream Burn wound its way through to the meanderings of Forth, where the heavy English cavalry could be bogged down and the dreaded archers isolated on islands in the bog.

What I am trying to say is that the novelist who has done his research and steeped himself in the characters – or at least his interpretation thereof – is quite as likely to have got it right as the cloistered academic who deals in quoted authorities. Moreover, since one of the novelist's primary preoccupations has to be the suspension of disbelief, in other words, to carry conviction, he may be the more likely to make fewer errors and *non sequiturs*. Put it this way, the professional historian may assert that he is concerned with facts, not inventions; but he tends to state *that* such-and-such happened. The novelist has to try to state *how* and *why* it happened, if he is going to make his readers accept his story.

Now this, to be sure, can carry its dangers and implies responsibility – for the reader may well come to believe a version which is contrary to that accepted by the history departments. How often I have had it asked by reviewers or put to me by interviewers, on TV, radio or at meetings – is this true history or is it history according to Tranter? I recognise the problem all too well – hence my preoccupation with integrity. I feel strongly that it is the author's responsibility, when describing people who lived and loved, sinned and suffered, to endeavour honestly and fairly to portray them, as in him lies, not twisting them for the sake of his story or convenience, not damning them out-of-hand because the history-books tend to accept them as villains or failures, not making any historical character act *out* of character. This can be difficult, I admit, and often I fail, I am sure. I have the cautionary example of the great Walter Scott ever before me, whom I much admire, but who damned Rob Roy MacGregor's name and fame, for future generations, by making him act totally out-of-character at the

Battle of Sheriffmuir, when he must have known that Rob in fact had no responsibility for that Jacobite disaster – on the contrary. You see, the historical novelist has this enormous opportunity, in that five hundred people may read his book for every one who will bother to read through straight history. The responsibility therefore is the greater.

There is another aspect of opportunity in the historical novel which is worth remarking on – the chance to put forward views which would hardly be acceptable in an ordinary modern novel or thriller – even if this does rather infringe the non-preaching rule. For instance, in the third of my Bruce trilogy, I was able to make quite a thing of the King's death-bed scene and there indicate some of my own thoughts and attitudes towards dying, death and the hereafter, using the dying monarch as mouthpiece. I felt that this was legitimate because of Bruce's own and known attitudes, his anxiety for his infant son David, his concern that his heart should be cut out and taken on crusade, in accordance with an unfulfilled vow, his acceptance that he would be punished hereafter as the excommunicated murderer of the Red Comyn, but his belief in ultimate forgiveness, and so on. Such a scene and exploitation would have been out-of-the-question in a novel of the present day; yet I had and still have a great many letters from readers all over the world dwelling on that scene and its implications, many of them exceedingly touching. Clearly it dealt with a matter of much concern to many. I could give numerous other examples.

Needless to say I became involved in so-called cultural activities other than the very private and alone business of writing for a living, with what someone called its inward-looking outlook, partly because I *was* a writer but also on account of my interests in Scotland's heritage from the past. On returning from army service I joined the Scottish Centre of International P.E.N., the writers' association and club – the initials stand for both *Pays Entre Nous,* and Poets, Essayists and Novelists. Quickly I got caught up in its activities, which were mainly social, admittedly, and the exchange of ideas, but which also covered concern over the writers' plight in certain countries less fortunate than ours, international 'together-ness' and the holding of Congresses in various world capitals. Writing being such a solitary life, it is good to meet fellow-practitioners and to compare notes, for older hands to encourage newcomers and to generally let the hair down. I enjoyed being a member of P.E.N., in due course became a committee-member, Junior Vice President, Senior Vice President and in 1962–66, Presi-dent. These stints of office were normally for three years each but sometimes for four, so I was involved in some responsibility for quite a long period. I don't suggest that my term of office was a specially momentous or fruitful one – I succeeded much more illustrious presidents like Eric Linklater and Douglas Young; but I did have some excitements and problems to face. Holding the International Congress in Edinburgh in 1951 was not the least of these. Controlling, if that is the word, four hundred-odd fellow-egotists from all over the world, determined on a holiday from

The Kyles of Bute, scenic excellence almost on Glasgow's doorstep

being respected citizens, can be trying, even taxing. Especially on the pocket, for these affairs have to be done in style, and keeping up with the international Joneses obligatory. Normally, of course, governments weigh in as a matter of prestige; but Scotland, a nation but not having a government of its own, was at a loss in more ways than one, the London government declaring that it had subsidised a P.E.N. World Congress in London only a few years before, and felt no responsibility to another in Scotland. We raised a fund from sympathetic contributors up here and put our hands deep into our own threadbare pockets, but this was not nearly enough to cover the costs of entertaining the four hundred for almost a week in the manner expected, and Scottish P.E.N. remained in debt thereafter for a number of years.

Lest the reader also gets the impression that P.E.N. exists entirely for parties and junketing, I would emphasise that such applies only to international congresses and the like, which most ordinary members never attend. Much good work is done throughout the year, in the cause of books and writing and the exchange of ideas. During my presidency, and since, I sought particularly to further the promotion of Public Lending Right, or the Brophy Penny as it was originally called. This is the scheme by which authors would be paid some small amount for books borrowed form free libraries. Public libraries and the free lending of books have become an accepted part of life, practically a social right. But the writers of the books have never been taken into account, *their* rights. A book may be issued a hundred times and more from a library, until it falls apart; giving much entertainment, enlightenment, or interest or sheer escapism to a great many readers; but the author benefits nothing, from all this. In fact, to some extent he loses, for some people who would otherwise buy his book naturally prefer to wait until they can read it for nothing from the library. When it is realised that the majority of hardback books sold are sold to libraries, something of the scale of the issue becomes clearer. John Brophy suggested that one penny be paid for the author each time a book was borrowed and this would have added up to a tidy sum when the many millions of book-issues were considered; but it would have involved considerable account-keeping and the librarians just would not contemplate it. At length the Public Lending Right idea was evolved whereby authors would be compensated for the number of their books on the library shelves. Again the librarians were against it – and there are many more librarians than authors! Eventually it was realised that since the libraries were a public service the government had a responsibility in the matter and should enforce it and pay something to make it work, out of public funds. Long years of pleading and lobbying have passed and time and again the thing has been brought before Parliament, always to be talked-out or dropped by an uninterested and three-quarters empty House. At last it did become alleged government policy, but the busy politicians never found time to do anything more about it – after all, the small numbers of writers' votes threaten no seats. The Society of Authors, the Publishers Association and the Library Association thrashed out a workable scheme and this at last was accepted by Parliament – although the amount of money suggested for its implementation will butter very little bread for authors, once the costs of administration are met and the publishers get their whack. That is as far as it has gone, the Mills of God far outstripping Westminster. Whether I will ever see a new penny from this source in my lifetime is highly doubtful. But future authors, if there are any, may benefit – for variations of the system have worked in other countries for years.

P.E.N.'s most publicised work has probably been its efforts to aid foreign writers oppressed by various non-democratic regimes, especially those imprisoned and otherwise misused behind the Iron Curtain. I well remember the mixed feelings I had when, in 1961, I had to act host to a group of a dozen Russian writers on an official visit, led by Aleksei Surkov, the poet and Chairman of the Foreign Commission of the Union of Soviet Writers, the so-careful talking, the pious platitudes, the skimming over very thin ice and the wary glances. I don't know that our efforts have achieved much, but at least we tried.

I was much affected when, in 1976 on the death of Sir Compton Mackenzie I was appointed Honorary President of Scottish P.E.N., which purely decorative but much-valued position I still hold, however inadequately.

With fairly typical rash impulsiveness, hardly had I relinquished my working presidency of P.E.N. when, with Lavinia Derwent, Jack House, the late Robin Stark, Ronald Johnston and others, I set about forming a Scottish branch of the Society of Authors. In case this may seem something of a duplication of effort, it falls to be pointed out that the two organisations have very different aims and functions. The Society is not a social club but a professional body concerned with writers' problems, conditions of work, legal questions, contracts, and so on. We felt that Scotland was too far away from the headquarters in London, however excellent these might be, and Scots members tended to be out-of-touch. I was made Chairman. One of our first activities was to establish the Meet the Author sessions annually at the Edinburgh International Festival, to try to give at least some small literary content to those proceedings. From the start it proved to be a success and has grown in size and scope down the years. At first we stuck to Scottish-based authors, not unnaturally, but in time the field has been widened. As a public activity, with books as well as authors on display, it has done much to bring writers out of their attics and corners and to make known their works, their methods of working and their personalities, to readers and those who may be tempted in. The *Scotsman* was a great help in getting this going. I suppose that I still consider that this public 'exposure' of authors is a good thing – although sometimes I think, and assert, that writers should be read and not seen. The reality does not always match up with the glowing mind-pictures conjured up by devoted readers, and the shattering disappointment may put the latter off the writer's books for all time! I remember the first time *I* met . . . ah, well better to let that flea stick to the wall!

Another allied effort was membership of the National Book League's Scottish Committee – of which, in course of time, I also

The author engaged in TV programme on castles

became Chairman, a seemingly inevitable process for which I cannot account for I am sure that as a chairman I must often infuriate my fellow-members. May used to say that it was as well that I was not a woman since I obviously couldn't say no. I suppose that it was partly, when I was trying to get ideas and projects pushed through, that it was easier to do so from the chair than from further down the table, especially against more cautious and probably wiser chairmen. The Book League, as its name implies, is concerned with the promotion of books and reading rather than the authors thereof, and does much good work, especially amongst young people and through institutions and colleges. Like so many of these committees, whatever achieved, the bonus for me has been the number of excellent people I have come to know and work with thereon, and who have put up with me for, so long. Mary Baxter, for long the organising secretary and now the Deputy Director for Scotland is a case in point. The amount of work she does for the book scene here, quietly and efficiently and with selfless devotion is beyond all computing.

Not all these cultural activities have been connected with books and writing. Very early on I joined the Saltire Society, and in due course took my turn as the Edinburgh Chairman. This admirable organisation is concerned with maintaining and exemplifying Scotland's traditions on almost every front. Nowadays its Saltire Awards for architectural excellence are deservedly esteemed; but this is only a very small part of its work. The late Rob:rt Hurd, whose driving-force was largely responsible for the Society's establishment and success, was an architect of renown; but his enthusiasm covered so much more than that. My interest in castles and towers drew me in, and I gained much more than I could contribute. It may be that the Saltire Society spread its support almost too widely, so that its impact became somewhat dispersed – I do not know. But if more people supported its aims, Scotland would be a better place. The Saltire, of course, is the national flag of Scotland, the white St. Andrew's cross on blue, not the red-and-gold Lion Rampant which is so often assumed to be but which really belongs only to the monarchy.

In 1966 I, with three others, established the St. Andrew Society of East Lothian, with similar objectives. We did not make it a branch of the Saltire Society, for by that time the Saltire had become rather typed in the public mind as 'middle-class intellectual' and we were anxious to base this new venture much more broadly – even though that description was quite unfair to the Saltire. The very broad base was necessary, the more so as our area of operations was so very narrow, a mere single county. From the start it was a success-story, with a large membership – larger than many national societies – drawn from all ranks and quarters of the population, although mainly centred on the county-town of Haddington. We carry out a regular programme of monthly events in support of things traditional, worthy and deserving of support in Scottish and rural life, indoors in winter with excursions in summer; nothing remarkable or too erudite, but determined not to be, as happens with some such societies, merely an annual-dinner affair – although we do make much of our St. Andrew's Night Dinner, to which we have been fortunate enough to attract a succession of the most distinguished speakers in Scotland, in the

The Adam Town-House of Haddington –
venue of the St. Andrew Society of East Lothian

fine Adam Town House of Haddington, over the years and which has become one of the highlights of the East Lothian season. After fourteen such years I fear that I am still the Chairman – which is bad policy and a weakness – although I have tried often to step down.

But enough of such involvements. Let me end this catalogue by declaring how much help and encouragement I have received personally, and for the projects in which I have been concerned, from radio and television. BBC Scotland comes in for a lot of hard knocks, but my experience of it, and of Scottish TV also, has been of much support, sympathetic consideration and courtesy. These cannot compete financially with the South, of course, and are therefore subject to many limitations. But they do much better than they are often given credit for, I am convinced, and I for one am appreciative. Scotland's cultural scene would be a lot bleaker without them.

chapter eight
TOWERS OF STRENGTH

There is one aspect of our heritage on which I could be a monumental bore if I was permitted – more so even than hitherto. That is, of course, on the subject of my old love, the castles, tower-houses and fortalices of Scotland. The subject itself is the reverse of boring, I hasten to add – that is the last thing one could say about these colourful, dramatic but functional and sturdy buildings, so full of character and often with a resounding history, in local if not national terms. It would be my harping on about them which might bore. So I must seek to restrain myself in this, the first and prevailing enthusiasm of my life. It was this, really, which pointed the way to all the rest.

I suppose that my schoolboy commitment was instinctive more than anything else. I do not remember anyone steering me in that direction. I used to cycle round the Lothians and Fife, to draw my castles, often peering over estate-walls or crawling through the grounds guiltily, in fear of lairds and gamekeepers, to find viewpoints from which to sketch – it never occurred to me to go and actually stick my neck out by asking permission. I fear that I was sadly indiscriminate, collecting almost as many sham castles and

Cawdor Castle, Nairnshire, 14–17th century stronghold of the Campbells

Victorian Scottish-Baronial reproductions as genuine fortalices. But in time I grew more knowledgeable and began to perceive a glimmering of the scope and excitement waiting to be uncovered – for this is the point; there was no *pro forma,* no convenient list of such places; and I soon realised that they were to be counted in their hundreds, even thousands. Macgibbon and Ross's *Castellated and Domestic Architecture of Scotland* was a treasure-trove, but not readily available then for such as myself – although it has now been republished, I am glad to say; also it had been written in the 1880s, in pony-and-trap days, and not unnaturally it missed out a good many examples and also described large numbers which sadly had since been swept away or fallen down. The official *Inventories of Ancient Monuments* were at that time strangely incomplete and only a few districts covered, although the areas being surveyed now are vastly better done. In my early days the field was vast and largely uncharted, and the excitment consequently the more challenging. I still have those youthful notebooks with their inky drawings and immature hand-of-write.

My aim in life then was to be a restoring architect. But family conditions and my father's death when I was at the stage of being apprenticed to an Edinburgh architectural firm, changed my direction, for I had to start earning money at once instead of embarking on a long-term educational course. I have often wondered whether this was a good or a bad thing?

I should probably explain something of just what these fortalices are and what makes them important. I am not dealing with the great military strengths and royal fortresses, such as Edinburgh, Stirling and Dumbarton Castles, nor yet early palaces like Holyrood and Falkland. These are well-known and with quite a different genesis and purpose. My concern is with the smaller, domestic fortified lairds'-houses, tower-houses, peel-towers, built between 1400 and 1650 – they are almost all called castles in Scotland – and which are unique to this country and an especial flowering of an individual architectural expression and national attitude.

Mains Castle, Dundee – now being restored

You may well ask, how can I state that, especially as to the uniqueness, when the Norman castle, the French chateau, the German schloss and so on are there, usually so much larger and more opulent, to rival them? Even the English moated manor-house. The answer is to be found in the national character and the historical situation. Scotland had comparatively few of the great Norman strongholds for the good reason that the Normans never conquered here, as in Wales, and King David's importees did not have to keep down a hostile population. But from the late 14th century onwards we developed a tradition of building sturdy stone towers – sometimes called peels, although that is a misnomer, the

Pitcullo Castle, Fife, restored from ruin

word peel being another form of pale or paling and referring to the curtain-wall round the courtyard and not the tower within – four-square, rising four or five storeys to a parapet and wall-walk, strong, with massive masonry of up to ten feet in thickness, slit windows, vaulted basements which could not be burned out, usually set within the said walled courtyards where was the well, stabling and so on, all with precious few embellishments and gestures towards gracious living. Little change in this pattern occurred until the late 16th century, although the L-plan developed from the square to improve defensive cover of the walling and save having to project the stair-well inwardly. No-one will claim, I think, that these, stout, authentic and even impressive as they were, actually constituted any unique architectural flowering. Then came James the Fifth's French queen, Mary of Guise or Lorraine, who for so long ruled Scotland for her infant daughter Mary Queen of Scots. She imported large numbers of French artists and architects as well as soldiers. Then, from 1562 onwards Mary, returning to Scotland from France, did likewise. And these, bringing their more lightsome and decorative French chateau flourish to our sturdy and no-nonsense Scots pattern of castle-building, produced the splendid, gallant and readily-identifiable fortalice-style which most experts agree is so much better than the sum of the two, and unrivalled elsewhere. The French, on their own, tended towards being overblown, just too much, wedding-cake architecture if you like; but married to our sternly functional strength this was counterbalanced and brought into proportion, the extravagances weeded out – for the Scots have always regarded effectiveness above all, save in government. So we acquired the angle-turrets and stair-towers, the dormer-windows and crowstepped-gables, the elaborate corbelling and string-courses, the decorative shot-holes and heraldic carving, the improved Z and E plans, which as well as making eminently defensible homes, as much required, with the improved internal arrangements and elementary sanitation, made for much less primitive living conditions whilst producing a delight to the eye and the aesthetic judgement.

Castle Menzies, Perthshire, being restored by Clan Menzies

All this was excellent, but two other factors came into play to ensure the precedence of Scotland, in this respect. One was that the rest of Europe, with the growth of centralised authority plus the advance in the effectiveness of artillery, largely outgrew the need and usefulness of fortified mansions. Not so in Scotland where, unfortunately or otherwise, the 16th and 17th centuries were the most unruly and lawless in all her history, the central authority seldom weaker. Add to this the fact that over half of the best land was in the hands of Holy Church, and when the Reformation came along, twenty years later than in the rest, all this land was confiscated and suddenly available to be parcelled out amongst a vast new class of landowners, younger sons of lords and lairds, prosperous merchants and tradesmen and the legal fraternity which arose out of the ruins of the old Church. This highly lucrative development was to be controlled, according to young James the Sixth, Mary's son, for the benefit of his own empty purse of course but also for the better order and policy of his realm, by him making

Menstrie Castle, Clackmannanshire, saved after demolition threat.
Typical late 16th century fortified house
as required by James the Sixth's legislation

it a condition of every grant of land worth over £100 Scots per year
– no large sum, even then – that the new owner built a 'tour of
fence' upon the said land, for the weal of the kingdom and the
shelter of the lieges from attack by the lawless. It did not quite work
out that way, to be sure; for once installed and snug in their fine
stone strongholds, the innumerable new lairds proved just as

oppressive as the old, and nobody could bring them to book, least of all King Jamie's most inadequate authority – and there were now an awful lot of them. It is hard to be exact in this matter, but I would estimate, from what remains, entire, ruinous, mere rickles of stanes and named sites, that there would be between four and five thousand of these buildings erected between 1560 and 1650, when the fortified-building period more or less ended. In fact, everyone who built a mansion, great or small, in Scotland during that most fecund period, built a Franco-Scottish defensive fortalice – it is as simple as that.

So there we have my challenge and joy – and sorrow also, to be sure, for so many of these irreplaceable assets of our past were at risk of demolition. It is not so much age and the elements which menace them, for they were so strongly built and with such thick stone walling that most can survive as respectable ruins at least, if vandals of all kinds permit. It is the zeal of local authorities for road-widening and housing-schemes which constitute the greatest threat nowadays – and Edinburgh, despite all its Festival pretensions, has been amongst the worst offenders – speculative builders also taking their toll. Another menace, of recent years, tending to invalidate the ancient monuments legislation aimed at protecting listed buildings, is the 'hazard to life and limb' conception, whereby owners of ruins and empty buildings fear claims by the public for the injury of children and youths climbing over the property and falling to their hurt. This neglect of their responsibilities by parents and others has resulted in many otherwise fairly entire castles being pulled down, with the consent of the authorities – a shameful commentary on our scale of values.

It was partly to try to do something about all this, though more for the sheer joy of the subject, that I wrote and managed to get published my first book, the aforementioned *Fortalices and Early Mansions of Southern Scotland 1400–1650,* this dealing only with the area south of Forth and Clyde. That was in 1935. Much more so, however, when I started my five-volume work on *The Fortified House in Scotland*, in 1962, with the aim of covering every such

Tilquhillie Castle, Kincardineshire, being restored.
Latterly used to house turkeys

building in Scotland, where the main features still survived; for in the interim so many of those described in the first book had gone. It was my hope that such a compendium, readily available at a modest price, would help to arouse public understanding of what a priceless heritage was at risk; to make it more difficult for demolishers to get away with it, through ignorance on the part of the public; and at the same time to encourage far-seeing and enthusiastic people to come forward to try to save some of the buildings; and to invest in actually restoring ruins to being livable-in houses again – for most of them are of moderate size, some quite small, and can be saved at not much more than the cost of building a modern bungalow, and when restored make the most delightful of homes, with the distinctive cachet which living in an ancient castle can bestow. I am glad to say that all three objectives had a measure of success.

It was a vast and daunting task, of course, demanding enormous research and enquiry and requiring us to visit every single parish in Scotland, searching, questioning, going down almost every private driveway to look and see whether old work was incorporated in later mansions. Inevitably we missed some – for since the fifth volume was published I have discovered perhaps a score more – I say we, because May was just as fully involved as was I, taking the notes and reading the maps for me as we drove, and interviewing the owners to get historical data and stories whilst I drew the rough sketches on the spot. I could not spare any large wordage for each house, of course, or the cost would have been quite prohibitive. 600 to 800 words each was the average, unfortunately, with about 120 castles to be described in each volume, dealing with them on a geographical basis, plus a pen-and-ink sketch. So I had to limit myself severely to a very brief description of the location, the architectural details and the merest summary of its history. The books became a standard work.

However, despite the brevity, there was enough included to attract many people to the idea of restoring; and naturally a large number wrote to me, and still ask me, over the years, to recommend possible and available examples. So commenced what has become one of the major satisfactions of my life – although also a tremendous time-consumer, inevitably, and pocket drainer – as a sort of unpaid marriage-broker between restorers and the restorable, for the saving of over thirty such fortalices where I may claim at least some responsibility. There may well be many others that I know not of. There are not a lot of experiences, I think, to beat actually sleeping as guest in a castle which only a year or two before was a roofless shell; and this has been more than once my happy lot.

Before more people start writing to me to find them castles to save, in sheer self-protection I should perhaps point out that there are other problems than the mere finding and financing. First of all,

Braikie Castle, Angus, unrestored but saveable

inevitably, a lot of the best bets have already been taken. Many which have not, are apt to be in the least attractive surroundings, in suburbs or near modern housing or factories, on top of fairly inaccessible cliffs, or in other remote situations where getting services and even an access-road could be difficult and expensive. Then there is the problem of ownership. Often these places are situated in private estates, superseded by a later mansion house and the owners, although refraining to do any restoring them-selves, do not want strangers coming to roost on their property. There are the lairds who will only give a lease, not sell – and not everyone wants to spend quite a lot of money restoring someone else's property. There are the farmers who have bought the sur-rounding land, who either do not want to see the ruins restored or ask too much for the privilege. And there is the question of escalat-ing costs – although, for that matter, escalating resultant values come into the balance-sheet also. It is not usually actual cost which is the stumbling-block.

Many of my 'clients' have had to consider half-a-dozen and more possibilities before they settled on their choice. I think that Marc Ellington, the folk singer from America, and his wife Karen went indefatigably round, more than anyone else that I remember, always coming back to me for more ammunition, before finally they decided on Towie Barclay in rural Aberdeenshire. This one had a specially fine interior, with magnificent great hall with minstrels' gallery and oratory, and I don't wonder that the Ellingtons fell for it. But it had one disadvantage. At some late stage the wallhead and parapet-walk had been lowered by two storeys, so that the massive tower looked unnaturally squat and out-of-proportion. When the restoration was finished, Karen and Marc asked May and myself to come and see it and stay overnight. When we were leaving, I told them how much we admired their determination and all that had been achieved. As a mere postscript, smiling, I remarked that it was just a pity that they couldn't have added on the missing two storeys whilst they were at it, and made it perfect – although that would have greatly increased the cost. Well, two years later when we were again in Aberdeenshire, we called to see the Ellingtons. And there were the two extra storeys duly built up within the parapet-walk, as I had sketched for them, the castle splendid again at its proper impressive height, and the Scottish saltire flag flying bravely above it. I was greatly chuffed.

Another indomitable individual is Peter Clarke, who also visited a great number of sites and even made one false start – which came to grief over problems with the owner – before settling on Powrie Castle near Dundee, an interesting place in that the courtyard area of the older keep had been developed most effectively in the late 16th and early 17th centuries and the keep itself allowed to go to ruin. This later two-storey range has many particularly fine features, and Peter has restored it all lovingly and now lives in it with wife and family. Whether anything can be done with the very derelict keep itself is a matter for speculation although there are plans. It is interesting and significant that both these youngish men have not been content just to rest on their laurels but have gone on to endeavour further as to the Scottish traditional scene, Ellington to republish, from Towie Barclay, ancient Scottish books long out-of-print; and Clarke to try to organise others in support of Scotland's heritage, on a wider scale.

I was particularly concerned about Fawside Castle in East Lothian, a large and imposing ruin, really two fortalices built together, on a hill-top site above the village of Wallyford near Musselburgh, with one of the most magnificent prospects in all Lothian. This was one of those cases where vandalism, and climbing children from Wallyford and Tranent, so worried the farmer-owner that he applied for permission from both East Lothian County Council, as it was then, and the ancient monuments people, to demolish – and, to my astonishment, obtained it. When I heard about this, I felt that something had to be done quickly. With the enthusiastic co-operation of the St. Andrew Society of East Lothian, I set up a Fawside Castle Preservation Committee and wrote letters to all and sundry in any way concerned, and to the press. We were fortunate in that Fawside was one of the places to which the Musselburgh cavalcade made an annual ride-out at the Honest Toun celebrations – a sort of Common Riding festival – and so we had the support of Musselburgh Town Council and the festival association, the Provost and Town Clerk joining the committee. The farmer, when we took the responsibility off his shoulders, was most helpful and joined the committee also. We managed to get a 'stay of execution' *pro tem,* but on the understanding that something was done about the danger situation. Masonry along the wallhead, loosened by the vandals and cast down, had to be made secure; and much internal damage having been done, the lower windows and doors had to be blocked up, hopefully, so that intruders could not get in. This was going to cost money, the hire of scaffolding, so necessary, especially expensive. So we set up a fighting-fund, the St. Andrew Society leading off, Musselburgh weighing in handsomely, and many individuals. Extraordinarily, we got £250 each from the County Council and the ancient monuments board, both of whom had given permission to demolish – a lesson to be learned here, surely.

So the preservation work went ahead. But of course this was only a palliative. The real answer was to find someone to buy and restore the castle in its entirety. But this was not easy, for as I have said it was a big place and it would be a very costly job. I sent a number of people to look at it, but all found it too large and too daunting a task – and I don't blame them. I did find one enthusiast who was prepared to tackle it, but it so happened that his father already owned a castle, which he would one day inherit, and he became persuaded that it was foolish to start on a long and major effort which might well not be finished when he found himself to have two castles on his hands. Then Tom Craig and his wife Claire turned up, who were not daunted and prepared to find the necessary funds to do it all properly, although not in haste. The plans are most ambitious and admirable, and before too long Fawside is going to be a most exciting and desirable residence again. It played a noteworthy part in the famous Battle of Pinkie in 1547, during the Rough Wooing of young Mary by Henry the Eighth of England. We read, from an English source, that the occupants of Fawside Castle shot at the invaders "with hand-guns and hakbutts till the battle lost, when they pluct in their peces lyke a dog his taile, and couched themselfes within, all muet; but by and by the hous was set on fyre and they, for their good will, brent and smoothered within". An English source, needless to say!

Mains Castle, East Kilbride, was an entirely different proposition, very much of a do-it-yourself effort by Mike Rowan, a young man of much courage, initiative and energy. Starting with a roofless square tower, with no floors remaining above the stone roof of the vaulted basement, with his own hands and those of his friends, over years of week-end and holiday work, he has restored Mains to habitation and regard once more. I doff my cap to Mike Rowan. There was an interesting TV feature on this restoration.

The saving of Rossend Castle in Burntisland, Fife, is quite a saga. It was in quite good and habitable condition until taken over, in the 1930s I think it was, by Burntisland Town Council, who wanted its land for municipal housing. For a while it was occupied as some sort of hotel. Then began its decline. The Town Council had no use for it nor interest in preserving it – indeed one of the provosts is quoted as calling it "an outdated monument to landlordism". They let its windows get broken and remain so. The vandals got in and little attempt was made to stop them, apparently. Year by year the condition of the castle deteriorated and presently there were the usual demands to pull the eyesore down. The Town Council was nothing loth. There were several efforts to prevent this happening, and demolition was postponed time and again. Twice there were appeals to the Secretary of State and temporary stays. I, and others, tried to get various agencies interested, the Saltire Society and the National Trust also trying. Rossend was not very suitable for a private house, situated where it was and large too. I wrote to the press and composed articles. We proposed its use as community-centre, local museum, eventide home etcetera, but without success. The Town Council renewed their decision to demolish. We redoubled efforts – for this was a very historic place and should have been the show-place of Burntisland. The attitude of the local authority was further exemplified by the remark made when the historical aspect was brought out "I would like to know what comprises historical? I understand Mary Queen of Scots stayed there one night – that's nothing to get hysterical about, never mind historical!" The Army was called in to demolish, but turned it down. At the last moment, after an abortive attempt to save it by an architect, Mr. Tony Wheeler, rescue arrived in the shape of Mr. Ian Begg, a partner in the architectural firm of Robert Hurd and Partners – the late Robert would have been pleased. Ian Begg, and colleagues in the Leven firm of Rolland and Partners, took over the derelict building for a small sum, not for any client but for the firm itself, to restore it and turn it into offices and workrooms for draughtsmen and so on. So now Rossend stands proudly again, whitewashed and kenspeckle on its knoll overlooking the town, something achieved.

Incidentally it should not be called Rossend at all, but Burntisland Castle. This was its name until in the 19th century when it

Rossend Castle, Burntisland, saved after long battle with municipal demolishers

Melgund that a local historian and writer, Jervise by name, had found a carved stone on the building bearing the initials D.B. and M.O. I could not find the stone, but then the place had become much more ruinous since Jervise wrote nearly a century before. Not, one might think, sufficient on which to base a large novel? But, wait. Such stones, carved with two sets of initials, are known as marriage-stones; and in all my lifelong experience of Scottish castles I have never known one *not* to relate to a marriage – and they are exceedingly common, most fortalices having one. Now Melgund was traditionally built by the notorious David Beaton, the Cardinal-Archbishop and Chancellor, or chief minister, of Scotland, who all but single-handed held up the Reformation here for some twenty years; in consequence the second most-execrated name in Scots history, after the False Monteith, the betrayer of Wallace. This was the D.B. Undoubtedly therefore the M.O. stood for Marion Ogilvy. This lady, daughter of the first Lord Ogilvy of Airlie, has gone down in history as concubine and courtesan, Beaton's 'chief lewd' to use John Knox's picturesque phrase, mother of Davy's large brood of illegitimate children, who between them are reputed to have built half of the castles of Angus. But, wait again. This was a *marriage*-stone, and such were of course never put up to mistresses and fallen women, however high-born. So, could Davy Beaton have indeed been married? I dug on. He was born in 1494, and after gaining his degrees in literature and philosophy at St. Andrews, seems to have acted as secretary to his uncle, Archbishop *James* Beaton, Primate and Chancellor for James the Fifth. Then he went to Paris, where he studied further, reputedly for several years, including divinity. So obviously he did not start out with the notion of becoming a priest, and seems to have entered holy orders as late as 1525, when he was thirty-one, when his uncle the Primate made him titular Abbot of Arbroath and Rector of Campsie, retaining half the great revenues of the Abbey for himself – Davy was still in France. It is therefore not only quite conceivable but almost probable that, high-spirited and handsome as he was, David Beaton had married Marion Ogilvy in earlier manhood and produced at least some of the numerous children. This seems the more likely when we learn that the said children were very much accepted as legitimate during their lifetime, marrying very well into the highest circles, one in 1546 indeed marrying, amidst scenes of great magnificence it is recorded, and in the presence of her father, the premier earl of Scotland, 10th Earl of Crawford. So we have the extraordinary situation where, in order to take holy orders and become, first, Abbot of Arbroath and then to succeed his uncle as Archbishop of St. Andrews, Primate and Chancellor of Scotland, Davy had to demote his wife Marion to the status of mistress or concubine, which promptly made all their children theoretically illegitimate – and in order to enable them to inherit his various properties, he had to go through the expensive process of legitimising them again, on sanction from the Vatican. All Scotland would know this at the time, of course; but it was Beaton's enemy John Knox, in his *History of the Reformation,* after Davy's murder, who damned his ex-wife as whore and concubine, chief lewd. Davy Beaton was scarcely a righteous man perhaps, and probably had very little true religion in him; but he was a patriot and the ablest Scot of his day. So you see why I wrote *A Stake in the Kingdom* out of what I unearthed at Melgund Castle.

I could give innumerable other examples both of intriguing historical finds and links which have been used in my novels, and of interesting, amusing or picturesque incidents in or about the castles themselves – as for instance when Mearns Castle in the Newton Mearns suburb of Glasgow, about which I was concerned, was restored as a church, the Kirk of Maxwell Mearns Castle, to my great surprise – and a fine chapel it makes. And the pit or prison of Udny Castle, Aberdeenshire, the fearsome hole in the thickness of the walling where the baron thereof had exercised his right of pit and gallows, which was turned into the most marvellous playroom for the restorers' children, only accessible by a withdrawable ladder from a trap-door in the flooring above; can you imagine the glee of the youngsters down there, ladder removed and able to cock a snook at all tiresome grown-up authority? Or Harthill

Mearns Castle, Renfrewshire, interior. Restored and now used as church

Udny Castle, Aberdeenshire, now restored after dereliction

Castle, at the back of Bennachie, in Oyne parish, Aberdeenshire also, magnificently restored after a lengthy search by another American couple, Ann and Stephen Remp, one of the very few where the gatehouse into the courtyard still partly survives and which was the seat of a lively family of Leiths. One, involved in the Montrose campaigns, seems to have been quite a character. Once, entering St. Nicholas Kirk in Aberdeen in the middle of a service, he insisted on taking the Provost's pew and on being offered another seat drew sword and swore "By God's wounds I'll sit beside the Provost and in no other place!" On being jailed, at his trial he asserted that the Provost was a 'doittit cock and ane ass', and snatching the complaint from the clerk-of-court, tore it up and casting the inkhorn and pen-holder in the clerk's face thereby 'hurt and wounded him in two several parts to the great effusion of blood'. Whilst new proceedings were being arranged, he tried to set the jail on fire, managed to arm the other prisoners and fired upon the populace. It is encouraging to know that this enterprising individual gained his release and went back to Harthill nine months later when Montrose again gained the mastery in Scotland. The present-day lairds of Harthill have much to live up to. Incidentally, this restoration won a Saltire Award.

But, as ever, I must restrain my garrulous pen. Let me end this chapter by recounting perhaps the oddest incident to occur to us, in visits to literally thousands of castle-sites over the years. Inchdrewer Castle, Banff, was taken and restored by one Robin de la Lanne Mirrlees, also called Count de la Lanne – I am not sure how he prefers to be described – owner I understand of sundry other houses in Europe and England. And may I say here that Inchdrewer, with which he apparently had family connections, taught me what *could* be done in the way of saving a building which previously I would have thought as beyond rescue. Well, the restoration not exactly finished but the castle at least wind-and-water-tight, the Count kindly invited me to a house-warming party there. I could not manage to attend, so he told me that next time I was in the area, I should call on his building-contractor in Banff, who had the only other key to the place beside his own – the Count was then living in

London – so as to inspect the work done. In due course May and I turned up at the builder's yard for the key; but that excellent individual insisted on taking us the three miles to Inchdrewer and showing us round, in person, rightly proud of what was being done. When we arrived at the only door – defensive houses are low on doors and entrances, with barred-up small windows – and the key was turned, out trotted a large white dog of the samoyed or chow type, in apparently excellent condition. It scarcely glanced at us and trotted off purposefully across the surrounding fields – Inchdrewer is situated high on a bare ridge with no other house nearby. Our builder-friend was both mystified and horrified. It was more than a week, he said since he had been up. Nobody else locally had a key and there was no other way in. So the wretched dog must have been shut in alone all that time, and without food or water – although how it had got in he could not imagine; he had never seen the animal before. The place would be in a fearful mess.

However, there was no mess, no smells, no signs at all of a dog's presence for a day, much less eight. Perplexed, after admiring all that had been achieved and hearing of future plans, we locked up again and left.

May and I largely forgot about that odd dog until, some months later, the Count sent us a copy of *Vogue* magazine, of all things. This contained an illustrated feature, very colourful, on his London house which had recently been redecorated with large and dramatic mural paintings, the significance of which is immaterial here. What did interest, however, was a brief paragraph at the end which mentioned that Count de la Lanne owned many other houses in various parts and had recently restored a small castle in Scotland, which was reputed to be haunted by a lady in the shape of a white dog.

Any explanations or suggestions? I may say that I am a very 'non-psychic' character, never having experienced any emanations, precognitions or anything of the sort, although May on occasion had had 'feelings' and awarenesses. And our Banff builder certainly did not strike us as a fanciful type.

So much for castles.

chapter nine
BY-PRODUCTS

My long preoccupation with castles has in fact enriched my life in many ways other than the obvious, and as providing material for historical novels. It took me into every corner of the land and opened my eyes to the infinite variety and richness in scene, character and tradition that was Scotland – a recognition which was to be amplified and exploited in my *Queen's Scotland* books. It necessarily got me interested in heraldry, for instance – for every castle had its heraldic panels, the interpretation of which could provide vital clues as to its story. Also in genealogy, an obvious by-product. And these two together led me into the study of titles and orders of chivalry, with consequent involvement. This in turn produced an interest in the idea of knighthood. And so on.

The Queen's Scotland idea did not originate with me. My London publishers, Hodder and Stoughton, had issued a very successful series, edited by that well-known character Arthur Mee of the *Children's Encyclopedia,* entitled *The King's England,* dealing parish by parish with all the areas in that fair land, by different authors. It was based largely on parish churches and was by no means exhaustive. Later, a Scottish version was started, with the one

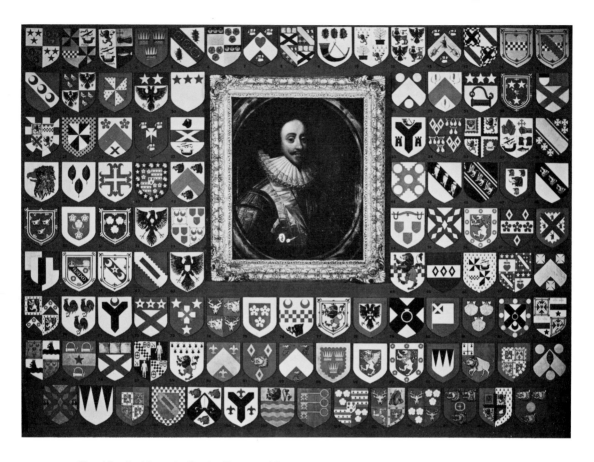

Heraldry in Menstrie Castle. Baronets' Room,
celebrating Nova Scotia baronetcies instituted by Charles First
on recommendation of William Alexander, of Menstrie, first Earl of Stirling

author, not an editor; but this got only as far as south of the Forth
and Clyde, plus Fife, before the writer concerned left the country.
Again, it was by no means exhaustive. The publishers, knowing that
I had finished the *Fortified House* volumes, asked me if I would take
on the large task of completing the series, and gave me a free hand
as to how I did it. This was in 1966, just after our only son's

accidental death coming home from a mountaineering expedition in Turkey, when May and I were in very low spirits and requiring some activity and interest which we might pursue together, a kind of therapy. And this seemed to be something we could do and which needed doing. For I visualised something very different from what had been done hitherto. Whilst working on the castle books I had been made all too well aware of the lack of any detailed guide to *all* the parishes, districts and areas of the land, describing all matters of interest, ancient and modern. There were gazetteers available, one in especial excellent, Groome's *Ordnance Gazetteer of Scotland* in six volumes, a valuable work of reference. But it could touch only briefly on items of interest and by no means all of those. On fortified houses, for instance, it was sadly inadequate. And it had been published in 1882, and much had happened since then. There were innumerable parish histories, usually written by some former minister, and many specialist books; but nothing comprehensive. I had already published *Land of the Scots,* a big 'coffee-table' book, profusely illustrated; but this was, as it were, skimming the cream, a mere skirmish with the subject. What was now intended was a really exhaustive work.

It proved to be exhausting too. Everything north of the Forth and Clyde, save for Fife and Kinross, was our objective, and we started with the most accessible area, the Heartland, the shires of Clackmannan, Stirling and Perth, a territory of about one hundred square miles. We quickly discovered how fascinating and exciting but how immensely time-consuming a task we had embarked upon. Despite all the necessary preliminary research, we were not long in being made aware of the enormous number of interesting and intriguing things to be discovered and described in even the most dull-seeming and humdrum parish, with every by-road and lane to be explored, every mansion and driveway to be dealt with, every kirk and kirkyard to be investigated – tombstones a major source of information and local lore – stone-circles, souterrains or earth-houses, chambered cairns, burial-cists and the like, as well as modern developments to cope with. The mileage we covered

Pictish Symbol Stone – note intricate relief carving

was phenomenal, the time-factor becoming ever more demanding. Admittedly, our hearts began to fail us at the thought of dealing thus with the far-away areas up in the north and west.

But there were many compensations, apart from the sheer satisfaction of learning about Scotland on the spot in depth and detail. *The Heartland* area particularly introduced us to the Pictish symbol-stones, that unique Scottish heritage which ought to be so much better-known and indeed made into a special attraction for visitors. These strange symbols carefully carved or incised on stone monoliths and dating mainly from the 5th to the 9th centuries, are still largely a mystery to scholars as to their meanings and significance, abstract designs of evidently great importance. There are about a dozen main symbols, only one of which is accepted as to its application, the mirror-and-comb symbol, which fairly obviously refers to women. Of the others, the double-disc and Z-rod, the serpent-and-Z-rod, the crescent and V-rod, the flower-pot and so on, the most challenging and picturesque is one called the elephant or Celtic-beast – although it is clearly no elephant, for the trunk or lappet of this strangely stylised and spirited representation comes out of the back of its head. These symbols are repeated by the hundred in different groupings, conveying some message unknown to us, all over Scotland; but most have been found in the main Pictish heartlands of Fortrenn, Angus and the Moray Firth area. There are excellent museum collections at Meigle in Perthshire (Fortrenn) and St. Vigeans in Angus. The Museum of Antiquities in Edinburgh has casts of many. May and I became great devotees of the symbol-stones and great was our joy when we came across an unrecorded one. Also exciting were the other Pictish carvings and ornamentation, especially the various stylised renderings of the boar, which remained the emblem of the royal house, Scottish as well as Pictish, until David's grandson, William the Lyon, adopted his lion rampant in the 12th-13th century. It is interesting that, with the advance of Christianity, these symbols, whatever they meant, were not suppressed but were incorporated in the cross-slabs and shafts; so their relevance was not obnoxious in any way to the Celtic missionaries.

Another feature which greatly interested us, and of which we had not previously heard, was the hog-backed grave-slabs of the early medieval period, whilst the Celtic influence still prevailed, massive stone coffin-shaped slabs with ridged tops, often intricately carved and decorated, for placing on top of a grave. Ancient churches too were apt to be full of interest, with their Pictish fonts often still in

Typical high pulpit kirk – the Word dominating all in Scots Kirk
worship. Blairdaff Church, Aberdeenshire

use today, their elaborately-carved sacrament-houses, their lep-
ers' squints and dramatic memorials. More modern ones too, with
their high pulpits, some extra-ordinately high, placed not at one
end as formerly but half-way down one side of the kirk, dominating
all – a sign of the emphasis of the Word in post-Reformation
Scotland, and one more indication of the Scots preoccupation with
theory, debate, metaphysics, in their ideas of worship.

But I go on. I must not spill out all these items of delight and
enthusiasm, new to us then. Suffice it to say that *The Heartland*
taught us much and left us eager for more – but also left us alarmed
at what we had taken on, the time it was going to take and the
inroads on our pockets.

However we went ahead with Aberdeen, Angus and Kincardine shires, for the second volume – and Aberdeenshire was a mighty labour, demanding weeks of travel, but a highly rewarding one as I have already indicated. Then the North-East volume, comprising the shires of Banff, Moray, Nairn, East Inverness and Easter Ross, a fascinating area also, although getting a long way from home. Finally we did Argyll and Bute, a tremendous task this because of sheer geography, sea-lochs and island-hopping, but of course with its especial compensations. I fear that we never got the remainder of the task completed – Caithness, Sutherland, Wester Ross and West Inverness-shire, nor yet the Orkney and Shetland Isles and the Outer Hebrides – for May's health had begun to break down and prolonged travel was no longer possible. Owing to the problems of finding overnight accommodation on these trips, we could not do them in the tourist season, so had to confine ourselves to spring, autumn and early winter. This, although it did give us freer roads and less difficulty with bed and board, also sometimes meant snow and ice, not to mention prolonged rain. And, a factor apt to be overlooked, long, long evenings to be passed in country pubs and chilly out-of-season guest-houses, with the light often making out-door activities impossible after say 5 pm. Ah, well – I suppose it was worth it all?

Anyone who has anything to do with history, especially local history, has to come to terms with heraldry sooner or later – for this is so often the clue, the essential key to open many a door into the past. And a fascinating study it can make, with much more to it than mere colourful design and romantic flourish. It is indeed called a science – although that seems to me to be overdoing it. There are all sorts of refinements and complexities – humour, too, in so-called canting heraldry. It started out as a necessity, firstly as emblems to be displayed on flags and banners to indicate, on the march or on battlefield, what prince or lord was here represented; as for instance the boar emblem of the Kings of Alba and Scots, the raven of the Norse and the plantain of the Plantagenets – how that family got their name. Then, as body armour developed and

Thistle Chapel, St. Giles, Edinburgh.
Notable for heraldic decoration of knights' stalls

became all-covering, features and identity were hidden and something was required to indicate who was inside all the steel-plating, in war and tournament. So personal signs and symbols became necessary for every knight, not only the leaders. Soon it was a token of gentility; and since coats-of-arms passed from father to sons, with marks of cadency and degree, genealogy and descent were also involved. This still obtains. Admittedly an element of snobbery may have crept in; but in fact anyone can apply to the Lord Lyon King of Arms for a grant of arms, which then becomes that individual's personal 'trade-mark' and cannot be infringed by others. Cities, towns, corporate bodies and even businesses can also register arms – although for myself I find the last incongruous. Incidentally, Scottish heraldry is recognised as perhaps the most 'pure' and unspoiled in the world, partly because it is a small country – although it is said to have more armigerous families per head of population than any other, thanks to pride of blood and concern for the past – partly because of the clan-system, which limited greatly the number of surnames used and so simplified heraldic invention; but mainly because of the legal powers and authority vested in the Lord Lyon and his Court, which are quite extraordinary and which prevents the unauthorised use or abuse of arms, as so prevalent elsewhere. In Scotland armorial bearings are a form of heritable property and so protected by law. Lyon King of Arms is a much more important and powerful person than his equivalents elsewhere, is in fact a Minister of the Crown and bears the honorific of Right Honourable, is not only one of the great Officers of State but ranks as a High Court judge, his person so sacred that to strike him is high treason! That in theory would allow him still to hang offenders – although I have not noticed reports of any recent hangings; fines are preferred. But he can still imprison for heraldic offences, can issue Letters of Horning or outlawry, forcibly erase unwarranted arms and 'dash them furth' if they happen to be on stained glass windows and the like, as was done at Glasgow Cathedral in 1862, and bogus County and Burgh arms removed from the Scottish National War Memorial in Edin-

what of the surname. Well, it seemed that for some reason not unconnected with spelling presumably, the Lethingtons of Salt-coats gradually changed their name to Livington; and from there it was but a short step to Livingstone, which was the family name of the Earls of Linlithgow and other *West* Lothian lairds. But their heraldry did not change. An example of the pitfalls of genealogy.

Heraldry, then, is the hand-maiden of genealogy, the history of families, a working knowledge of which is essential for any writer of historical novels. I have been criticised as too much concerned with genealogical detail in my books – and perhaps there is some-thing in that. But so much of history can be a complete mystery and even nonsense without an understanding of relationships and descent that really I do not feel that apologies are called for. Anyway, I always include a list of principal characters, in order of appearance and with brief genealogical indications, at the front of each book, for bemused readers. As example of the need for genealogical exactitude I cite my Bruce trilogy. The history-books usually state baldly, in their take-it-or-leave-it fashion that Thomas Randolph, later Earl of Moray and Regent of Scotland for the infant David the Second, was Bruce's nephew; as was Sir David de Brechin, who rebelled against him but was forgiven. Certainly Randolph, although a foe to start with, later rallied to the hero-king and became one of his principal lieutenants. But, nephew? Bruce had four brothers and three sisters. None of the brothers left legitimate offspring, and Mary Bruce was not married; Christian was married three times, but not to anyone called either Randolph or Brechin; and Isobel was Queen of Norway. Randolph was almost as old as the Bruce brothers anyway. So who was he, and Brechin? It was Professor G.W.S. Barrow who provided me with the clue, in his excellent book on Robert Bruce, pointing out that Bruce's mother, Marjorie, Countess of Carrick in her own right, before she married Robert Bruce of Annandale, had been wed to a brother of the MacDuff Earl of Fife, the Lord Adam of Kilconquhar and by him had had daughters, one of whom married Randolph of Noddsdale and the other a de Brechin. So the offspring of these matches were grandchildren of Bruce's mother and therefore half-nephews of the King. The text-books were right, in this instance, but did not explain.

The idea of knighthood and orders of chivalry had long intrigued me, since it was obviously so intensely important to our ancestors. For instance, what do you make of it when you read that at the Battle of Agincourt (I think it was) the Earl of Surrey, unhorsed by a young Frenchman, picked himself up to find the other's sword at his gorget. Clearly he would have to yield, or die; but before doing either he demanded of his assailant whether he was a knight? On being told no, the Earl ordered his captor to kneel, there and then, on the battlefield, and dubbed the young man knight with his own sword before yielding it up in surrender. This illustrates more points than one. It was obviously vitally important and below the dignity of a knight to yield to a man not of knightly status. Also that knighthood is not a matter of rank but of personal status, in that this lofty earl was content to yield his sword to some undistinguished young man so long as he was a fellow-knight, so had to be made one. Again, that the conferring of knighthood was not a prerogative of the monarch only but inherent in knightly status itself; in other words, any knight can in theory create another knight, and only a knight can do so, kings themselves having first to be knighted before they can lawfully create others. In practice however it was usually only great noblemen and commanders in the field who were apt to do so. Most evidently there were many misconceptions about knighthood abroad.

What really set me off investigating this subject was again one of the little failures of the text-books, which a novelist had to try to rectify if he was going to carry the necessary conviction. The historians refer to William Wallace before the great Battle of Stirling Bridge but *Sir* William afterwards. Who knighted Wallace, then? There was certainly no available King of Scots to do so, and most of the great nobles hated Wallace as an upstart, indeed most were on Edward of England's side. Again it was Professor Barrow, a historian after my own heart, who provided the clue. Rishanger, he revealed, an English chronicler of the period, declared that Wallace had been knighted by one of the great earls of Scotland. This information was perhaps less meagre than it seemed; for of the great earls of Scotland at that time only two were at all likely to be in a position to knight Wallace or to wish to do so – the exceptions being Lennox and Carrick. Now the Earl of Lennox, descendant of a long line of Celtic chiefs, was a somewhat doubtful character, reasonably patriotic of intent but weak. He had, like most of the others, if against his better inclinations, come to terms with the occupying English. He started the Battle of Stirling Bridge on the English side; but when he saw that Wallace was going to win he discreetly transferred himself to the other side – to Wallace's scorn. Do you imagine that William Wallace, the idealist, the man noble above all others in his conception of honour and right, arguably one of the greatest Scotsmen who ever lived, would have knelt to accept the honour of knighthood from a turncoat and craven? It is inconceivable. So that leaves Carrick – who was of course Robert the Bruce himself. He was not present at the battle but holding the South-West in the patriotic cause. It seems probable that *he* knighted Wallace, at Selkirk a little later, when the victor of Stirling Bridge was appointed Guardian of Scotland – as was entirely suitable.

That quest and others similar led me into all sorts of byways on the theme of knighthood, which I found as absorbing as it was valuable in my work. I learned too about the orders of chivalry, which although much older as an idea, had been established mainly during the Crusades, with especial duties and objectives. So I discovered that there were two forms of knighthood – knights bachelor, that is those created *ad hoc* as it were, individuals honoured for services rendered or on account of some personal excellence; and members of knightly orders, national or international, usually also admitted for merit or outstanding service, but not always so. Here is no place to go into these matters. Let it suffice to say that the idea of knighthood has worn fairly well down the centuries and, of course, survives today, as a much-sought-after honour, especially in this United Kingdom – where, I fear, its application is often shamefully prostituted. Politically-motivated Honours Lists, and the almost automatic knighting of big business tycoons and top civil servants, are a grievous misdirection of what should be a very special acknowledgement of particularly valuable services to the nation and society, not some sort of reward for financial contributions, departmental prestige or long service. For knighthood is essentially a distinction, a promotion in status, not a title conferred – it should be as much an honour for a prince-of-the-blood or a duke to be made a knight, as for anybody else. And it bears a religious significance as well as a social one – for the admission to knighthood ceremonies ought to include a vigil and vow-taking in the sight of God. I fear that most of our present-day knightings are far from that conception. Of the British orders only the Thistle and the Garter, so far as I know, still conform in some measure to these standards – the others are largely mere classifications. The international orders tend to do rather better in most cases. I am glad to say that the Military and Hospitaller Order of St. Lazarus of Jerusalem, to which I had the great honour of being admitted in 1961, as Knight Commander, still insists on a religious service of initiation, and expects Christian beliefs and behaviour from its members. This order was founded as long ago as 1098, mainly to aid in the fight, amongst Crusaders, of the dread disease of leprosy; and the relief of leprosy is still its foremost aim, together with forwarding ecumenicity in Christian affairs. It is interesting to Scots that Alexander the Third appropriated the revenues of the burgh kirk of St. Giles and its Grange, in Edinburgh, to the Order of St. Lazarus, in 1286, the year of his death, a renewal of David the First's grant.

I suppose that it may seem a bit far-fetched to assert that all this followed from my interest in castles. I daresay that I might have come to much of it anyway, in time. But I know that it was because I had written the castle volumes, and had to visit every parish in Scotland to do so, that Hodders asked me to tackle the *Queen's Scotland* task – and it was that which really introduced us to the

St. Monans Kirk, Fife. Founded by David the Second in 1362.
A stern Scots metaphysical statement in stone

Picts in a big way and the Picts which led on to some study of the
Celtic Church – a subject which I feel has been sadly neglected by
Scottish academics and students, yes and clergymen also. For over
four centuries, after all, it was the *only* Church in Scotland; and its
beliefs, attitudes, direction, rituals and buildings have helped to
make the Scots what they are, and should be an essential study in

our universities and colleges. But I must not get started on *that* pet theory, at this late stage. Anyway, I shall hereafter end up with some words on religious outlook, the supernatural and metaphysics generally – for those who will still bear with me.

Finally I would like to wind up this chapter on by-products with an acknowledgement of an aspect of the castle and *Queen's Scotland* books which I have not so far touched upon. That is the friendships which we made in the process and which have been a great joy to us. I shall not go into details, but just say how much richer our lives have been made by the association with, and the kindness and affection shown by, so many fine folk, to whom I say thank-you with all my heart.

As postscript, it will not have escaped the notice of readers that throughout I have said little or nothing about that most significant area of Scotland, the Orkney and Shetland Isles, for reasons that seem adequate to me. I *know* the rest of Scotland – with the exception perhaps of the Outer Hebrides – but to my undoubted loss I do not know Orkney and Shetland. I have been in Orkney – I had to go there for my castles – and could rhapsodise over St. Magnus Cathedral, the Bishop's and Earl's castles, the character of the islands and the islanders, and so on. But I do not claim to really know the very special features, circumstances and ethos of these Scandinavian-orientated islands and am in no position to write about them with any sort of awareness. I have never visited Shetland, alas, although I ought to have done. I herewith apologise.

chapter ten
THE IMMATERIAL

Arising out of much that has gone before, I feel that I ought to say just a little about this matter of metaphysics, religious theory and practice, faith, the unseen and so on – after all, more Scots have enthused and struggled, fought and died, for these and allied causes than for almost any other, a preoccupation deeply embedded in the national consciousness, however superficially bashful we are about talking of it in these modern times.

I have spoken of the genesis of it all, in the sun-worship and the stone-circles, of Celtic Christianity, of the impact of the Roman Church, of the Reformation, the Bishops' Wars, the Covenanters and the Killing Times, all of which have inevitably left their mark on the nation and its subconscious. Until quite recently the Scots were notably a church-going people – for reasons which may not always have been of the highest and most acceptable to their Creator but which, by and large, were worthy, concerned with worship and standards. Today all this has changed and only a minority attend church with any regularity, and the younger folk most evidently absent – although Sunday-schools still flourish, as some token gesture towards religion by the children's parents.

St. Magnus Cathedral, Kirkwall, Orkney.
Scots ecclesiastical architecture at its best

Also, I would think, the average Scot still expects to be classed as Christian, and takes it for granted that the Church will be available for marriages and funerals – all this, I suggest, still less worthy than the popular accusation about folk going to church in the past for wrong reasons, out of habit and social pressures.

Basically then are the Scots no longer metaphysicians and concerned with the ideas of truth, reason and belief, the unseen, eternity and the rest? I think not. I do not believe that it is possible for a nation to change so entrenched an attitude and character in the course of a generation or two. Other aspects of the Scots character have not changed much, so why should this very basic one? I think that the transcendental is still there, not dormant but actually suppressed – and if so, there will be a price to pay. No essential part of our nature and make-up may be suppressed for long without an eruption of some sort, as our history should have shown us, warned us; and something extreme is usually the outcome, which would be a pity.

You see, all mankind is essentially a worshipping creation – and by their very nature the Scots especially so. Men require to wonder – which is an especial aspect of worship – to recognise, however dimly, a force and intelligence greater than themselves. God indeed help us when we cease to do that! In every age and every race the search goes on for something which will answer the questions, something which will make sense of current follies and wickedness, something beyond our rather absurd and feckless selves who have made such a mess of things, which will add up to ultimate sanity, order and security. Do not tell me that the Scots, of all people, have lost interest in that?

I claim to be a Christian – a mighty poor one, a back-slider and broken reed, but a Christian of sorts. I believe, as do most of us if we allow ourselves really to give an honest answer, that Christ unmistakeably and for all time showed the way, nearly two thousand years ago. Unfortunately, being men and women, we have been squabbling over *our* interpretation of Christ's way ever since – and nowhere more vehemently than here in Scotland. God, the ultimate answer, whatever name you give him, must indeed shake His head over the so-called crown of His creation. Yet, if man is made in the image of God, as Christ taught, then perhaps He would rather that we squabbled and got worked up over it all than ignored Him and shrugged Him off entirely, or couldn't be bothered. I know that *I* would, one of the cracked and very half-baked images of God – and I suspect that you would, too.

So, then, what are the Scots doing today about the eternal verities, love, truth, order and beauty? Since, for once, we are not fighting about them. They are there, undeniably. They exist. Man has neither invented them nor can of himself do more than recognise them. These are the proofs of the existence of a mind and being and authority infinitely greater than man's – and uncomfortable matters to consider if you are not going to try to do something about them, however little. Today the whole world is groping, feebly, almost blindly considering the guidance which has been before us all for so long, but ever more frenetically, for at least truth and order, even if it tends rather to overlook the other so essential two, love and beauty. Never have there been so many weird religions and cults springing up, such an interest in the occult, in sham astrology and horoscopes, in witchcraft and necromancy and the like, so many press articles on spiritualism, faith-healing, TV programmes on poltergeists, life-after-death and so on. Even the preoccupation with space-travel and wars-of-the-stars and that sort of juvenility is symptomatic of the same need, a basic recognition and reaching out towards the unseen, the something beyond us.

As a churchman of sorts, I admit that the Church, in all its too many branches, is largely failing to satisfy this incoherent need. That certainly is not all the Church's fault. It does try, or some of it does. Recently I was invited to address a week-end conference organised by the Church of Scotland's Department of Education, at Carberry Tower – incidentally another excellent use for an ancient fortalice – on Contemporary Spirituality, a distinctly offputting title but a vital aspect of this subject. My own contribution was very feeble and superficial, I am afraid, being mainly concerned with the

Carberry Tower, East Lothian. Former seat of the Lords Elphinstone, now a Church of Scotland conference centre

secular writer's attitudes and responsibilities in the matter; but listening, I heard much that enlightened and enheartened me. Those taking part were by no means all ministers, and there were many young people. These were Scots groping for answers in the age-old tradition although in very modern terms, and eager to do something about it.

We are always being told that we live in a materialistic age; but I take leave to doubt whether this age is any more materialistic in essence than any other, and considerably less so than some. A lot of the 19th century was a lot more materialistic than this, I quite confidently assert, as was much of the 18th. It seems to me largely a question of the public face as against the private concern and uncertainty, of superficial media-fed attitudes and underlying basic doubts and fears. Now doubts and fears, in their place, can be no bad things – however foreign to accepted Scots character – so long as they do not altogether inhibit positive decision and action. I suggest that this is largely what is wrong today in this aspect of Scottish life, as in others. Owing to instant communications, air-travel, mass-media, multi-national corporations and influences as well as centralisation of government, the world seems to have become so much smaller, yet omnipresent to us all; and Scotland and the Scots an ever tinier part of it. We tend to feel ourselves overshadowed, no longer important in the scheme of things, no longer capable of affecting or effecting anything very much – in other words, we are in what is glibly called a crisis of confidence, something the traditional Scots ought not to know if they are to remain true to themselves. We have forgotten perhaps, temporarily, that size is not the criterion, that it is usually the small peoples who change the face of the world – the Jews, the Greeks even the Romans, none large nations, who really set the pace.

So, I say, if the Scots can get over this unnatural lack of their accustomed confidence, they have still a great contribution to make to the spiritual well-being of their fellow-men – and in the process, do themselves a power of good. In the past we have been something of a power-house, on the ethical and intellectual front.

We could and should be so again. I think that quite possibly we shall, for, as I say, you don't change a people's basic character and driving-force overnight. The Church in Scotland today, in its various branches, is certainly more aware and awake to its failures and opportunities, as well as its problems, than it has been for long – a most hopeful sign.

I see more than the Church as having a major part to play here – I see the universities. I must say that I am disappointed in Scotland's universities. For so long we largely led the way in this aspect of national life. When England, with ten times our population, had only Oxford and Cambridge – giants, admittedly– we had four, St. Andrews, Glasgow, Aberdeen and Edinburgh. And they were dynamos indeed, generating intellectual energy and advancement of thought and knowledge, which was felt far outwith Scotland. Incidentally, we almost had a fifth, for in 1592 a royal charter was issued to erect a university at Fraserburgh, the building was actually erected but for some reason the scheme fell through – although the building was occupied as such for a little while, when, in 1647, owing to plague in Aberdeen, King's College removed there temporarily. Today we have eight, with Heriot-Watt, Strathclyde, Dundee and Stirling added – which is still a much greater proportion per head of population than in most countries; but the current seems to have run down somewhat, the drive slackened. We no longer lead the world, I fear; just as our less advanced education in schools and colleges is no longer held up as an example, as it used to be.

Why? Partly the same crisis of confidence, I suppose – and since the universities train the school-teachers, the responsibility for the latter must in large measure lie with the former. But is there more than that? I think that there must be, some malaise of identity which did not formerly afflict them. Some might blame the technological aspect, the concentration on the practical, the scientific and the manipulative, at the expense of what used to be called the humanities. Others may say that these institutions have become something of degree-factories instead of true universities, con-

St. Andrew's University – the oldest in Scotland

Stirling University – new, but surely unsurpassed in its scenic setting

cerned more with training students for the labour-market than with advancing fuller living. Others again that universal education up to entrance standards was bound, through sheer weight of numbers, to overload the boat and reduce pace and performance. There may be something in all these. But I suggest that what might be called the cultural nationalist aspect must be looked at. I am only too well aware that learning and knowledge is no suitable sphere for political theories of nationalism; but the fact remains that our Scots universities have become very largely anglified in the last decades, in direction and outlook, in senior staff and in some cases even in the student body. Any glance at statistics will confirm this. Now, whilst this may have no ill effects on standards of learning and instruction, even have a widening influence, obviously it can have a very real effect on basic identity and outlook in the institutions themselves. I am not suggesting, as in other respects, that being essentially Scottish is any better than being English, Welsh, Irish or French – only different. Today, our centres of higher education are not really Scottish universities any more, but just universities. Whether this is a good thing or a bad thing is not the point. What is undeniable, I think, is that this change in emphasis and identity has affected all Scottish education and therefore Scottish life. And since we live in an era in which mass and non-Scottish influences are ever increasing anyway, this vital one has to be considered and not brushed aside as mere nationalist prejudice. I admit that it is probably too late to turn back the tide now; but at least we ought to recognise what has been happening to us on the shore. No doubt this process has been happening in other lands too – but here I am concerned with Scotland.

All this may seem a long way from my starting-point, the seeming Scots retreat from metaphysics and religion. But since the leaders of the nation's thought, in Church, bureaucracy and education, are trained in our universities, I do not think that we should underestimate their influence. I am nowise slamming the universities, for I recognise that they have to cater for the times, to cope with conditions as they are, not as we might wish them to be. They are under heavy pressures. I have had considerable kindness from some of them; indeed Edinburgh was kind – or rash – enough to bestow on me an honorary degree, for which I am suitably grateful. I am only pointing out trends and consequences.

So, then, are the Scots going to become more and more anglified and less and less concerned with considering the whys and wherefores in preoccupation with the hows and whats? Not that I suggest that the one follows from the other! Personally I am inclined to think not. The need to probe and enquire and dispute, to split hairs if you like, is too much part of us. This leopard may be lying very low, almost hibernating indeed – but it will not change its spots; and one day something or somebody will arouse it and it will commence to emulate a lion rampant again. I do not say that the churches will necessarily be full once more, that missionaries will stream out again, that the universities will be transformed; but if not, some other manifestations of worship and wonder will emerge to meet the Scots' need and urge – and others will no doubt benefit. All history says so, and history seldom fails to repeat itself.

This, probably, is as good a place as any to wind up – if not well past that point . . . !

EPILOGUE

I started out by saying that I never wanted to live anywhere else but in Scotland – and that stands, despite all the flytings and vilifications, the grumbles and pontifications and holier-than-thou opinions expressed herein. All the criticisms apply just as much to myself as anyone else.

What then of the future? I am an optimist, I suppose, in most matters. I see Scotland surviving – but only just managing to retain its essential character; that is, if mankind as a whole survives current follies and threats. But even so the Scots will survive as some sort of special identity. Do not tell me that the Creator has made anything so odd, awkward and individual, just to let it evaporate or fizzle out hereafter, either for nuclear or less dramatic reasons. I do not say that the Scots will necessarily have their own star in the firmament of heaven somewhere – as we were alleged to have our own ark at the Flood – a difficult and contrary planet it would be, probably orbiting in the opposite direction from all the others; but I feel that since recognisable individual human character will assuredly survive into eternity, so probably will national character, or some aspect of it. I do not believe that our Maker goes to a lot of trouble to make such things and then forgets or abandons them.

As to specific problems, I think that the Scots will achieve some form of self-government sooner rather than later – in sheer instinctive self-preservation. Whether we will make any better job of governing ourselves, is another matter, but I hope so. I believe that we shall experience a return to a more overt spirituality, using the phrase in its basic sense; and will again have the nerve to act the missionary towards less enlightened folk – that is, everyone outwith Scotland. I accept that we are bound to have agonising times ahead of us still – we will make them for ourselves and deserve them. But at the end of it all we shall still be the Scots.

Here's tae us – wha, God help us, is like us?

Nigel and May Tranter in the garden of their home near Aberlady

The timeless, unchanging challenge of the high places, which has helped to mould the Scots character – Stac Polly in Wester Ross

CASTLE ILLUSTRATIONS BY THE AUTHOR

ACKNOWLEDGMENTS

The publishers wish to thank the following
for the photographs which appear in this book
George Morice: pp. 12, 30, 45, 86, 87
James W. Murray: p. 174
The Scotsman: pp. 74, 77, 104, 144
The Scottish Tourist Board: pp. 10, 15, 23, 24, 26, 36
38, 43, 53, 55, 56, 57, 59, 63, 84, 95, 97, 101, 115
118, 121, 127, 129, 131, 152, 155, 157, 161, 168, 170
177, 178, 184
Nigel Tranter: pp. 18, 21, 35, 41, 81, 107, 125, 132, 134, 135
137, 139, 148, 159, 183

LIST OF ILLUSTRATIONS